ARE
WE
ALL
CANNIBALS?

This book uncovers and illuminates the origins of insecurity like none other. It leads the reader to every truth that is needed for true inner security. Every ministry leader needs to read this book. Every Christian needs to read this book. Every human needs to read this book. A life changing ride from performing and competing to a deep assurance and security as a true child of God. This book will quietly demand surrender as it makes one thirsty to live in our original design. I can't overstate what this book did for my personal development as a follower of Christ. It gets to the core of social human behavior and compels the reader to live like they were designed. In full relationship with their Heavenly Father.

Tony Froese, Founding Pastor & Teacher
New City Church

This book is a must-read for anyone searching for that closeness and stability with God that they still haven't found. Page after page offers insight into who we are as humans and how we so often misinterpret the world around us, falling into patterns of behavior that lead us further from the security and relational faith offered to us through the Father. David's book offers a way back. To freedom in who we are as individuals and ultimately to the Father's warm embrace over us as His kid.

Sarah Brandt, Teacher, Blogger and Author of Blossom Like Eden

David Braun speaks and writes not simply as one who knows *about* Father God, but as one who *knows* the Father. I was able to observe him up close, in person, when he was going through some of the experiences described in this book. I know that the temptation was very strong to conform to the pressures to become somebody that was not his true identity in Christ. He has been contending to see the Church of Jesus Christ reflect Him more as a *family* than as an *institution*. David has come through the fire refined as gold, and reflects so much of what the heavenly Father is like, not only in his own personal life, but in the lives of his family members who all have a message for this fatherless generation that God is a good, good Father.

Roger Armbruster, Director, Canada Awakening Ministries

Are we All Cannibals is a must read for all believers. I've had the privilege of serving with David in Youth with A Mission and have learned much from his teachings. David's understanding of the Father heart of God in this book left me knowing Him better and a desire to know much more. David writes from personal experience and personal study. Get ready for a deeper walk with your father as you read this book.

Randy Thomas, Former base Director & Pastor
Youth With A Mission, All Nations Institute

Are We All Cannibals is a guiding light that clearly articulates how deep and dark our orphan brokenness is without the revelation of adoption. David shows us the steps, not just to freedom, but to family. We learn that this process involves unmasking lies with the truth… the fullness of who and whose we are! When we feed the orphan pain, we live so far below Abba Father's heart passion for each of us. Then we, His children, cannibalize ourselves and others. To think that He provides not just Protection, but Belonging, Provision, and Significance just makes this God too irresistible to comprehend. David sets the table by drawing us into the longing of the Father step by step. Get ready, the journey out of orphan shadows and up into sonship is transforming! This is not an easy read. This is not a hard read either; it is a must read!

Duane Siemens, Lead Pastor, Certified Life Coach
The Wave Church

I just finished reading the last chapter of Are We All Cannibals. I was brought to tears throughout when reading the intimate and brave vulnerability shared. This book will sweetly and deeply impact its readers. I most appreciated David's vulnerability when sharing his life story and journey. The book's biblical teaching interspersed throughout with transparent sharing of David's personal times of crisis were very relatable. Are We All Cannibals provides intriguing breadcrumbs to a path of discovery and hope, for all who are hungry for more.

Betty Hutchens, Former Director of Pastoral Care

As I read through the pages of David's book, I heard the whispers of Father God speaking revelation straight to my heart. I realized I didn't have to scale any mountain to find God, He was right there with me. This book lays out the truth that's always been there, but with a fresh perspective and model for learning that lends an easy path into personal understanding.

Joel Brandt, Business Owner, Sales Manager and Entrepreneur

ARE
WE
ALL
CANNIBALS?

**Experiencing God's Security
in a World that Devours
One Another**

DAVID BRAUN

ARE WE ALL CANNIBALS?

Copyright © 2021 by David Braun

Unless otherwise indicated, scripture quotations are taken from the Holy Bible, New Living Translation, copyright © 1996, 2004, 2007 by Tyndale House Foundation. Used by permission of Tyndale House Publisher, Inc., Carol Stream, Illinois 60188. All rights reserved. • Scripture quotations marked (NIV) are taken from the Holy Bible, NEW INTERNATIONAL VERSION ®, NIV® Copyright © 1973, 1978, 1984, 2011 by Biblica, Inc.® Used by permission. All rights reserved worldwide. • Scripture quotations marked (AMP) are taken from the Amplified Bible, Copyright © 1954, 1958, 1962, 1964, 1965, 1987 by The Lockman Foundation. Used by permission. • Scripture quotations marked (TLB) are taken from The Living Bible copyright © 1971. Used by permission of Tyndale House Publishers, Carol Stream, Illinois 60188. All rights reserved.

Printed in Canada.

ISBN: 978-1-7776325-0-2

eBook ISBN: 978-1-7776325-1-9

ATN Press

Box 639, Niverville, Mb., R0A 1E0

Cataloguing in Publication information can be obtained from Library and Archives Canada.

Visit the author's website at www.areweallcannibals.com

Svea Braun—you are my greatest cheerleader, confidant and friend.

I could not have completed this without you.

Dad and Mom—thank you for living a life of celebration, sacrifice, and connection.

To my Daughters—you inspire me with your creativity, loyalty and zest for life.

TABLE OF CONTENTS

INTRODUCTION

Are We All Cannibals?

Have you ever had a disturbing conversation?

I have, with Jesus.

In 2010, I was disturbed and challenged by a dream I believe came from God. In the dream, Jesus said several things to me, but one stood out. With tears in his eyes, he shared, "David, my people live as social cannibals, feeding on each other rather than filling their hearts with me."

As I woke up, dazed and shocked, the meaning of this dream pressed on my heart. Cannibalism is the practice of eating another's flesh. Ritual cannibalism is sick and inhumane. It desecrates people made in the image of God. Social cannibalism is stealing another person's life for our own temporary satisfaction. We *use* people to gain life for ourselves. Our insecurities lead us to feed on others through deceit, gossip, manipulation, defensiveness, control, slander, gloating, judgment, and even passive-aggressive withdrawal.

Suddenly, "backbiting" and "backstabbing" took on a whole new meaning for me. So did the apostle Paul's scathing admonition to the Galatian church:

For you have been called to live in freedom, my brothers and sisters. But don't use your freedom to satisfy your sinful nature. Instead, use your freedom to serve one another in love. For the whole law can be summed up in this one command: "Love your neighbor as yourself." But *if you are always biting and devouring one another, watch out!* Beware of destroying one another. (Galatians 5:13-15)

I was convicted. My whole life, I had casually engaged in "tearing up" and "feeding on" people around me, people I knew and even people I didn't know personally. Jesus had said he was the Bread of Life (John 6:36), and yet there were so many times I felt justified in nibbling on someone's reputation because I didn't agree with their theology, life decisions, or behaviors. I believed I was right and they were wrong, so I just kept on biting.

In the weeks that followed, the more I considered Jesus's words, the more challenged I became. Jesus invited his followers to take Communion, that is, the breaking of bread and sharing of wine Jesus instituted at the Last Supper (Matthew 26:26-29; 1 Corinthians 11:23-26). He said, "Do this in remembrance of me" (Luke 22:19) as a celebration of his body and blood, which gives spiritual life.

In first century Rome, Christians were marginalized, maligned, and martyred as actual cannibals for answering Jesus's invitation to practice Communion. Yet in the present day, how easy it was for me to go through motions of eating bread and drinking wine (or the modern counterpart of crackers and juice) and then feed on my friends and neighbors in the church parking lot. My life looked something like the following.

"It's been an okay week. On Sunday I heard a decent sermon and took Communion. On Tuesday, someone misjudged my character at work, ripping off part of my hand. It was excruciating, but surprisingly there was not that much blood. On Wednesday, my soul was so hungry. Thankfully, we had our small-group supper, where we discussed and carved up our pastor, eating a good chunk of his leg meat. He was predictably tasty. I love it when pastors and politicians are wrong. It makes for a fascinating dinner party.

"By Friday I was ravenous again (could be the cold weather). Anyway, I lost my temper with my kids and spent the evening micro-managing them towards perfection. I only took a nibble of their necks just to tide me over. I got my fill, though, on Saturday at the hockey game with my brother. I spent the drive home backbiting my wife. Didn't realize she had that much meat on her back."

This may sound crude, and maybe it is. But the fact is that all our souls are hungry, and the only satisfying answer is Jesus Christ. The reality is that a soul feeding on anything other than Jesus has degrading results. This reality is wired into our biology. Science has found that the same regions of the brain that register physical pain such as a cut or broken limb also register emotional pain. So I can actually punch you in the stomach with my fist *or* my words. Whoever said "sticks and stones can break my bones, but words will never hurt me" is just flat wrong! And the science shows acute emotional pain lasts far longer than physical pain.

I have always considered myself to be a gentle guy and would never consider physically attacking another person. But I've been far too willing in word, deed, or thought to cannibalize my fellow human beings. How far did the impacts of this brokenness go?

After this dream, I began to see social cannibalism everywhere I looked. As a pastor, I saw it Sunday morning, in leadership meetings, and everywhere in between. As a town councillor serving my community in public office, I saw it in coffee shops, community hall meetings, and on street corners. As an organizational consultant, I observed it throughout the week between board members, managers, staff, and employees.

These observations had a powerful impact on me as I came to realize social cannibalism is like a deadly virus, feeding on and destroying individual trust in relationships, families, and churches. What's more, I could see people cannibalizing (feeding on) their successes, failures, and even their own bodies in ways similar to alcoholism and drug addiction.

Social cannibalism is real and has devastating consequences. It is for this reason I felt called to write *Are We All Cannibals?* As I will explain in the following chapters, Jesus did not come just to save us from hell or get us into heaven after we die. His death on the cross, burial, and resurrection were meant to transform our existence while we are still here on Earth (2 Corinthians 5:17; Philippians 1:6). He escorted you and I into a new reality where experiencing protection, significance, provision, and belonging are the norms for our soul. As the Father's children, we should be free from any mindsets blocking us from the banquet of security he has for us every day (Romans 12:2).

I quickly found that when I was not feeding on the Bread of Life (John 6:35), I easily slipped into starvation mode and found myself tempted toward social cannibalism. As you read this book, my desire is that it will help you see areas of your own life starving for security and fulfillment. My hope is that it points you to the real source of life. But before we start, may I share my own journey of craving and seeking fulfillment? This will help you understand why I would ask, "Are we all cannibals?"

CHAPTER ONE

Setting The Table

The first in a family of five children, I was born in London, UK, in 1973 to two loving Canadian-Mennonite parents. My parents were committed Christians, in England for my father to attend London Bible College. As he shared with my mother right after my birth, he had an immediate conviction of what my name should be.

"He is to be called David, I'm sure of it, because like the biblical King David, he is to be a man after God's own heart!" (1 Samuel 13:14; Acts 13:22)

Within days of my arrival, my father wrote out a one-page prophetic prayer of commissioning in the back of his Bible. This prayer declared my life to be marked, like King David, with a special call and desire for God. Even as a boy, when my father told me of his spiritual experience writing this prayer, I quietly pondered what this all meant for my life.

I was less than a year old when my father graduated from London Bible College. We flew back to my parents' hometown in Manitoba, a province in central Canada. The town was a small prairie community of about sixteen hundred residents. There I enjoyed a peaceful, sheltered childhood. While no parents are perfect, mine were amazingly supportive, engaging, and mature. We enjoyed laughter and conversation over our evening meal and a weekly family night set aside for movie-watching, sports, hiking, or just joking and talking over good food. There were camping trips and the odd vacation. In short, my parents knew how to have fun and enjoy their children.

My mother was an incredible listener whose sensitive, gentle heart made her a safe place to confide all my internal treasures and fears. For most of my growing-up years, we struggled to pay bills, however my mother's highly-organized, frugal budgeting skills carried us through many difficult financial situations. My father was an outgoing, encouraging, and authentic dad who deeply loved God and his family. He would often say that if your Christianity did not include laughter, it was missing something real.

In 1980, my father was invited to be the senior pastor of a growing, vibrant non-denominational charismatic church. The church eventually grew to a weekly Sunday attendance of three hundred congregants. I remember sitting in the services as a boy, feeling the warm connectedness of our church community and being stirred by stories of healing and salvation. Well before my teen years, I was exposed to many valuable lessons in hearing God's voice, standing on his Word, and the power of God's love to heal, forgive, and set free from physical and emotional bondage.

Despite these great community influences, oversensitivity, self-hatred, anxiety, and timidity dominated my internal world like a disease. I was petrified of people and situations. As early as grade one, my teacher contacted my mother concerned for my mental and emotional adjustment. I was so nervous that if my parents left me in the car to pop briefly into a store or neighbor's house, I would crawl down into the floor space to hide, worried that someone might kidnap me. Though I had a loving, supportive homelife, I could be terrified by almost anything.

MY FIRST COURSE—MEETING JESUS

I had invited Jesus into my heart when I was four years old, but it was a few months after my twelfth birthday when I experienced a real spiritual awakening. Over a period of six months, my heart started burning to truly know who Jesus was. I would read or listen to any Christian material I could get my hands on. By this point, my dad had experienced a personal crisis, burned out and stepped down for several years from pastoral ministry. At the same time, I was thirteen and my own internal hunger to know Jesus was at a peak.

I eventually encountered Jesus in a most peculiar way. You may have heard some interesting testimonies of places where Jesus met people—walking on water, at a wedding, in dreams, strip clubs, near death experiences (you get the picture!). My life was turned upside-down when Jesus met me personally sitting on my tuba case.

It was a Friday night during the fall of 1986. I played tuba in our high school band. I'd taken my tuba home for the weekend to practice. That Friday, I'd just come home from youth group and was reading my Bible. I'd been reading through the book of Luke and was finishing the account of the crucifixion and resurrection when I suddenly felt God's love touch me so deeply that I began weeping. It was awesome!

After at least half an hour of this, I felt impressed to look up. There next to me at waist height, I saw—whether in my imagination or a vision—Jesus sitting on my tuba case smiling at me. In those moments, I experienced his love with an intensity I'd never known. The simple message impressed on my heart was: "David, I love you, I'm with you, and I've called you to something special."

You can imagine this had a profound effect on me. Following this encounter, my heart lifted with a new hope and confidence. But though my confidence sky-rocketed, deep down I felt big holes of insecurity. While I was good at sports and didn't struggle with my studies, I avoided sports and academia throughout high school, getting involved only in situations where the pain of insecurity could be ignored or minimized. At this point in my life, I knew confidence but not deep heart security, something I'll expand on later.

Amidst those situations, many doors began opening for me to lead worship and travel in ministry. By the time I was sixteen, I'd been on five missionary trips to central Mexico. I'd led prayer meetings, preached sermons, seen God's miraculous power at work, and even delivered a message to Canadian youth on the steps of Canada's legislative capital. In my personal life, I was deeply experiencing Jesus's love in my devotional times. How sweet and transformative it all was! Yet below the surface, insecurity still ravaged me to the point that I regularly skipped brushing my hair because of the deep disappointment I felt looking in the mirror.

MY SECOND COURSE—MEETING THE HOLY SPIRIT

When I was twenty, my father rejoined our church leadership as senior pastor. Then at twenty-one years of age, my "ministry" identity broke apart after a series of disappointments hit me. This included a car accident, experiencing a business failure, having my home church leadership stumble, and my high school girlfriend breaking up with me. My confidence gone, I felt alone and uncertain about everything.

But it was also during this difficult period that I first met the Holy Spirit as my best friend and life companion. This occurred while I was reading a book describing the Holy Spirit's beautiful, tender heart. Once I experienced this awakening and recognized his existence in my life, I was certain I would now live in the peace and purpose I'd been lacking for so many years.

What followed over the next couple decades was a growing reliance on God and a growing outflow of ministry impact. During these years, I was privileged to see God heal people's physical or emotional brokenness. Hundreds received Jesus as Savior. I helped start a leadership school and planted a church in Mexico City.

> I had developed unconscious, ineffective mindsets for managing my insecurities.

Yet throughout this period, I unconsciously tolerated a life where insecurity remained a regular and dominant part of my internal world. Of course, everyone encounters insecurity. Some of us are less aware of its impact on our decisions and behavior. As an overly-sensitive person, I was constantly aware of insecurity but had not found a permanent solution for it. I had developed unconscious, ineffective mindsets for managing my insecurities. As I eventually learned, these mindsets had not been revealed and tested by true crisis.

As I will share in the next few chapters, nowhere did my personal insecurity, timidity, and anxiety affect me more than in relationships with myself and others. I yearned to find a life partner but struggled with starting and maintaining relationships with various wonderful Christian girls in whom I was interested. In 2000, I graduated with degrees in conflict resolution and psychology. In 2001, I joined a YWAM missionary campus in Colorado to receive Bible training. It was there I met and married my beautiful wife (more about this later on). In 2003, my new wife and I moved to central Canada to pastor with my dad in the only church I had ever consistently attended.

MY THIRD COURSE—MEETING FATHER GOD

Upon our arrival, we were received with great warmth and encouragement from so many congregants, friends, and relatives. As a third-generation pastor serving in my childhood church, I had every reason to feel confident. My wife Svea, and I joyfully served full-time on a part-time stipend, living in my parents' basement for the first year to make ends meet.

Although we enjoyed many wonderful relationships and had meaningful ministry experiences as youth pastors, then later when I served as administrative pastor, I found myself feeling quietly uneasy about everything. I was never able to savor rest. I constantly felt my vulnerabilities, weaknesses, and insecurities in the teams I led, the relationships I had, even the sermons I preached.

Early in our pastoral assignment, I knew I wasn't called to be our church's future senior pastor. Yet expectations quickly grew into assumptions about my future role among many well-meaning people in our congregation, some of whom were relatives and prominent leaders of their own ministries. While feeling the weight of these growing expectations, in 2005 I formally notified core spiritual leaders in our church of my intentions not to assume a permanent leadership pastoral role. I did so again in writing in 2008 and once more in 2010. In each case, my voice was acknowledged but not acted on, so the pressure continued to build. While I loved my church community, I knew I could not meet their expectations.

During this same period, there were also huge blessings. My wife and I started building our own family when our first daughter was born in 2005. We went on to have three more daughters in 2007, 2009, and 2011. We delighted in our time together as a family and forming our own family traditions. Trips to visit my in-laws in California were special highlights.

In 2008, I was invited by a fellow student from my university days to engage in adult training opportunities for a business he had started. From 2008 to 2009, I was graciously released by my church leadership a couple days a month to lead training and consulting opportunities for government and business. This helped expand my knowledge of what gifts God had placed in me. It also provided tuition for me to do distance learning at the University of London in the UK, from which I graduated in 2010 with my Master of Science in Organizational Psychology.

During these years, I was also honored to serve a four-year term as a council member for our community. Several prominent business and political leaders approached me about running for mayor. Outwardly, it seemed as though I was experiencing a lot of success. But I could feel a storm gathering in our church community and leadership.

It all came to a climax in 2010 when my father, who had served continuously now as senior pastor for almost two decades, resigned. This was followed in 2011 by my own public announcement to our congregation that I didn't feel led to move into the vacant senior pastor role. With our church growing, talks of a building expansion, and my demonstrated abilities to preach and administrate, stepping into my father's shoes just seemed logical to many congregants. Unfortunately, though I'd been transparent since 2005 that I didn't feel called to this role, church leaders had made no preparations for this time of transition.

So why not just resign from my pastoral position? Though tempted to leave, after much prayer I felt God guiding me to remain for the present as a bridge from where we currently were to what God had in mind for our church community in the future. Unfortunately, there were three major storm clouds colliding above me I didn't fully understand at the time.

First, no functional organizational guidelines or church constitution had been established by our founding church leaders to give direction on making a healthy leadership shift. Because of rapid growth prior to 2010, expectations of continued expansion remained high. But within months of my dad's resignation, uncertainty birthed gossip, polarization, and fear. The congregation was slowly sinking into misunderstanding, conflict, and fragmentation.

Second, since this was my childhood church, I enjoyed great favor as church members had witnessed my maturing as both a believer and leader. Many of them unconsciously assumed my life's call was to be their senior pastor with some even believing God had spoken to them of what my place was to be within the future of our church leadership. I was deeply torn as I didn't want to disappoint or be misunderstood by life-long friends and family.

Third, due to some historic messy leadership transitions in our church's thirty-five-year history, no one was willing or empowered to step into a position of senior leadership once my father resigned as senior pastor. Because of this leadership vacuum, it seemed to my anxious, insecure heart there was no telling how long or turbulent the next chapter of our church family life would be. The result was a crisis speeding up by the week, spinning out of control, a "perfect storm" of social cannibalism with me in the middle of it. I hit a major wall physically, emotionally, mentally, and spiritually, and I just could not move past it.

Finally in the summer of 2011, I had an encounter with God as my heavenly Father that revolutionized my life (as I will share in more depth later), satisfying my life-long hunger pangs of insecurity. Over the months following this encounter, my newly-growing relationship with my heavenly Father began drying up long-standing insecurities and anxieties. I remained as an unofficial "transition pastor" from 2011 to 2013. Meanwhile, the situation in our church continued to deteriorate as rumors, conflicts, and character assassinations ran rampant. Many people left.

Still, during this same period I was able to teach on identity, the kingdom of God, and who our Father God is. I felt so free and secure as I led prayer and fellowship times among staff and leadership. I was able to forgive and honor those people who misinterpreted my motivations and decisions and in some cases attacked my character.

By the end of 2013, God beautifully reconciled relationships and raised up mature leaders, resulting in a healthy church community that to this day relates effectively within the membership and to the town. By 2015, God released Svea and I from our church leadership position. This launched our family into an exciting faith adventure of teaching the Bible at mission schools, Christian camps, and church retreats. I also moved into marketplace consulting for organizations in government, finance, and telecommunications.

Today our church community is stronger than ever. I, in turn, rejoice in continuing the life-long discovery of what it means to live as God's son, full of security, joy, and purpose.

YOUR NEXT COURSE?

May I invite you now to take a few moments to consider what "foods" could be currently satisfying your hunger for acceptance, significance, and provision. Are those foods healthy and nutritious or just sugar-and-chemical-filled junk food? As you move through this book, you will get a chance to look at ways of exchanging those spiritual "junk foods" for deliciously nutritious and tasty "treats."

At the end of each chapter, you will also find a short section that reviews the key takeaways of that chapter, a few reflection questions to help you apply the chapter to your own life, and a prayer you are free to use in directing your heart to God.

In the coming chapters, we will explore four different types of identity mindsets full of cannibalistic tendencies. When we fail to relate with Father God to meet our basic human needs, these dysfunctional mindsets can subtly creep up even to the point of adopting them into our personality and daily habits.

We will also explore how connecting with God as our Father can effortlessly replace these four cannibalistic mindsets with four new, more powerful mindsets and behaviors reflected in who Jesus was and how he lived on this earth. I call these new "God" mindsets and behaviors Impact Drivers. At the end of this book, I include an abbreviated introduction to a tool I call the Impact Styles Inventory as well as some additional online resources to help you understand yourself better.

For instance, do you ever feel deep insecurity or anxiety about a relationship with a family member, colleague, business, or church situation? Do you ever find that no matter how many times you pray, read Scripture, or listen to your favorite worship songs, you are not truly at rest? By that, I mean a rest where your mind relaxes because emotionally it feels that your problem is already dealt with even though nothing outwardly has changed.

Or do you feel as though your life is drifting aimlessly, pointlessly? Presumably when you were growing up as a child, you didn't plan on your life getting stuck in quicksand. Maybe there is a person or group of people you try to avoid at all costs. If so, why? Do you feel a vague, constantly pulsing worry that your needs may not be fully met socially, emotionally, physically, or financially? Does the world around you seem a dangerous jungle, threatening you and causing you to live in a constant state of hyper-vigilance?

I could go on, but I don't have to because I know that for me and most likely for you, the answer is "yes" and "yes." If that is the case, I'd like to invite you to journey with me. As you do, I pray that in these pages your senses will be opened to understand a new way of satisfying your own personal hunger for security and fulfillment.

MY HOPE FOR YOU AS YOU READ

From my experience, the last thing we need is another list of supernatural dos and don'ts for breaking free from ugly realities. But what I want to share with you is amazingly simple. It cuts to the core of who you are and who God is. If you will just read these pages with an open heart, I truly believe you will find an incredible unlocking of internal peace. I've seen it happen before. I've experienced it myself. We can learn together how to effortlessly, peacefully, and powerfully move beyond past limitations and the crazy cannibalism in our world. We can move to an amazing new reality that was always meant for you.

So, as you read through my humble attempt to share some of the eternal breadcrumbs I've tasted, I sincerely hope that in some small way you may encounter some of the wonderful benefits I've experienced.

- In the middle of challenging situations, I'm experiencing an increased calming security, detaching me from the outside "storms," regardless of how personal they feel.

- I'm growing in an unshakable sense of knowing who I am, which in turn fills me with a deep sense of being known and cherished all the time.

- I'm continually expanding my joy levels and adventuresome openness to taking risks with a playful view of the future.

- Regardless of the challenges in my life or situations from the past, I live with a hope and sense of purpose and vision for my future.

- I've greatly grown to love relationally "dangerous" people rather than feeling threatened by differences, relational conflicts, agendas, weaknesses, or volatilities.

- I am continually growing into an out-of-this-world security, which allows me to live vulnerably, happily dealing with the unknown while enjoying the true authentic me.

REFLECTIONS

- We all have a life story which has affected who we are today.

- It is possible to meet and have a relationship with God and still be unfulfilled, anxious, or alone.

QUESTIONS TO CONSIDER

- What have been the major internal challenges you have struggled with throughout your life?

- How would you describe your emotional connection to God?

CONNECTING WITH MY FATHER

May I invite you to join in the following prayer with me.

"Lord, I want to know more of who you are and all the things you want to be for me. I believe you are the only one who can show me more of who I am. I invite you into my story. I invite you to touch my heart. Please show me your heart for me in those times in my life where I've missed your best. I reject regret. I thank you that there is so much more you want to give me. I welcome you to show me the way. In Jesus's name, amen!"

CHAPTER TWO

Rescued

*I*n 2011, the unfolding church crisis, I described in the previous chapter, had left me broken, exhausted and desperately needing help. During this period, my family took a vacation to visit my wife's parents in California. While there, I heard of a conference for church leaders. An offer of free counselling and prayer ministry caught my attention.

With expectations low, I arranged to leave our kids with my in-laws so Svea and I could attend the conference, and I could receive some additional counselling sessions. Sitting in the counselling center lobby, I stared at the day's date, circled like a big round eye on the calendar behind the receptionist: June 28, 2011. I felt it staring back, mocking me. The second hand on the round, white wall clock clicked rhythmically forward. *My life has passed by so quickly!*

I hated waiting in lobbies, especially this one. The pale-pink plastic flowers, laminate fake-marble countertop, worn carpet, and bare walls crowded in, making me feel trapped. *Is this really a good idea? Can this really help?* The suffocating weight on my chest pressed in more acutely.

Backed into a corner by fear and anxiety, I knew that if I didn't find a breakthrough, I was heading for a breakdown. I had pastored a church, led mission trips, witnessed God's power transforming lives. Yet here I sat, the nervous and fragile David Braun. This was hardly where I'd imagined myself a decade earlier when I'd returned home from Bible school overflowing with confidence that I'd lead our church to maturity and explosive growth.

Ten years later, neither had happened. My plan had always been to move on from my hometown after a few years, possibly to an international mission assignment. That had never happened either. Instead, after declining to take my father's place as senior pastor, I'd seen my church descend into social cannibalism with my own dignity, reputation, friendships, and personal life the main course on some menus. Ten years of striving to do my best, preach my best, serve my best, and give my best hadn't been enough. I felt alone and abandoned.

Bottom line, I was a mess, stumbling under huge mental stress, unable to eat or sleep properly. There were nights where my physical heart ached so much I wondered when my first heart attack would hit. In the swirl of so many voices and opinions, division and conflict, I groped for self-protection, trying every prayer, declaration, or verse I'd learned over previous decades to carve out some place of mental and emotional safety. But the feeding frenzy raged on, and I could find no relief.

"Okay David. We're ready for you."

The words jerked me back to the present. Shoulders sagging, I moved towards the open door. I felt empty. I knew all the pat theological answers for finding a breakthrough but they weren't helping me now. I'd heard God's loving voice and known his gentle touch. Yet something was missing. Something that kept me going around and around the same mountain without ever ascending it. My past excitement in God was now only a memory, leaving a gnawing emptiness, frustration, and anxiety.

How do I find peace? After ten years of serving, will I only be remembered for what I didn't do for my church?

As I entered the counselor's office, a small window cast shadows like a silent audience across the floor. The room already held two occupants, a tall, lanky, middle-aged man and a petite, dark-haired woman. The man thrust out his right hand, curious, friendly eyes peering through dark rimmed glasses. "You must be David. Nice to meet you."

Shaking my hand, he gestured me to sit in a slick, black armchair just under the window. As I took a seat, the woman gave me a warm smile. "Welcome David. Thanks for joining us. It's our honor to stand with you in prayer over the next couple hours. In a few minutes, I'm going to ask you to close your eyes and share what God shows you."

She gestured to her companion. "Is it okay if my colleague takes notes of what you share? Whatever you share is confidential, and all notes will be given to you to review and pray about."

The woman then described the process of listening prayer, where we would prayerfully ask God a question and wait for his response. She explained that God's communication to me might include my imagination being filled with truthful images (Philippians

4:8) or my emotions filling up with peace, joy, or love, which are fruits of the Spirit (Galatians 6:22-23). Or God might also bring a Bible verse, story, or worship song to my mind to communicate his heart for me. She added that I might also feel physical sensations of awe, the way one gets goosebumps when seeing the Grand Canyon for the first time.

She finished by explaining that listening to God's communication was a natural experience. We then all bowed our heads, and the counselor prayed, "God, what do you want to show David today?"

After pausing a couple minutes, she gently asked me, "David, what's coming up for you right now?"

As I sat there in my chair, my heartrate gradually descended into peace. My anxious thoughts soothed into silence, and I felt a warmth and safety wrapping around me. The years of built-up tension were evaporating. I kept my eyes closed. Something inside of me knew God wanted to show me I wasn't alone, and with this fresh awareness of his love, a flicker of renewed hope sparked inside. Having grown up in an expressive charismatic church, I'd experienced God in many different ways and thought I knew all there was to know, but this was something different.

With the eyes of my imagination, I saw the figure of a man standing in front of me. Smiling eyes looking into mine. *This is Jesus, the Son of God!* I knew immediately. What got me was how casual he was. His hands were in the pockets of his jeans, as he leaned to one side, a slight, almost mischievous grin on his face. He leaned toward me, giving me a quick poke in the side to make me laugh.

"You can be so serious!" he chuckled, "I love and care for you. You mean so much to my heart, bro!"

Still carrying the vestiges of distant fear, annoyance, and suspicion from moments earlier in a different world, I sputtered with rigid awkwardness, "Jesus, what do you want to do for me today?"

His firm hand gently grasped my shoulder. "Follow me, and I'll teach you a non-conventional way."

I followed Jesus. We moved off a highway, passing through a field with tall, brown grass, through thick bushes, and down a steep, narrow path. As we reached the bottom of the path, sounds of roaring water drew my eyes to a calm, blue lake with a torrent of water falling on the other side. The sight of it made me thirsty but also reminded me of the choppy waters within my heart.

Jesus pointed playfully to the water. "Have a drink."

Bending down, I cupped my hands and took a drink. The cold water seeped into every pore of my mouth and throat, filling my being with a wave of refreshment. What followed was an almost full-blown belch. Waves of joy and happiness bubbled up. Looking up at Jesus, I grinned like a five-year-old who has just tasted cotton candy for the first time.

With a broad smile, Jesus said gently, "This is the river I've placed inside of you."

Gazing in wonder at the water, I asked, "Am I in heaven, Jesus?"

He flipped a stone into the water with his toe. "Yes and no. I have placed heaven inside of you. So yes, we are in heaven. But no, this is not the full experience of the place I am preparing for you because right now we are in your heart."

"My heart? Like in my body?"

"Not your physical heart. We are in the center of your inner being. The place where you make conscious choices, have memories, experience affections, thoughts, imaginations, feelings, hurts, and hopes. This is my most cherished place."

I looked around in admiration at the beauty. A thought struck me. "So is Father God here too?"

Jesus pointed to the top of the cliff where the water poured over into the lake below. There, a distant figure stood waving. I somehow knew this was Father God and felt immediate awe. What was he like? Though I'd studied and even preached about the Trinity, and my prayers often began with "heavenly Father," I had only a vague grasp of who Father God was.

I was about to turn around, thinking I'd explore the shoreline with Jesus. Maybe he'd show me some cool things. But just then I heard the call of a deep voice from across the water. "Come on up here!"

Squinting up more carefully, I saw that the figure on top of the cliff was a broad-shouldered man. Bobbing next to him in the rushing torrent that spilled down over the cliff was what looked like a yellow dinghy. Curiosity bubbled up in me. *Is that really the Father of all? What is he like?* I had to go up there!

I'd no idea how life-changing my encounter would be. My credentials were solid. I'd been a Christian for thirty-four years, in full-time ministry for at least twelve. I'd seen much, done much, and thought I knew much. But really, I knew nothing. I had known *about* Father God, but in reality, I'd never met him personally. What happened to me in those next few moments went down deep into the core of my being and still ripples through my life today.

I headed toward the cliff wall, but it loomed high and steep, rising at least two hundred feet. Climbing it was way beyond my abilities. Dismay rolled over me like a cloud. But of course Jesus is the best rock-climber in the world, right? After all, he can move mountains!

Stumbling along, I followed Jesus, learning to climb past my fears and overcome the obstacle in front of me. Although there were a few close calls, sweaty hands, and quivering muscles Jesus's strong grip pulled me upward over ledges and precipices. He guided my footholds, and whispered encouragement through my fear.

Finally, I heaved my belly up onto grassy level ground and rolled over onto my back. Pulling me to my feet, Jesus looked into my eyes. "David, I want to introduce you to our Father."

> Father God was more amazing than my wildest dreams and completely unlike any preconceived pictures that had filled the void in my imagination.

I turned and, in that moment, felt known as I'd never been known before. Father God was more amazing than my wildest dreams and completely unlike any preconceived pictures that had filled the void in my imagination. A strong, handsome, muscular, bronze-skinned man with broad shoulders stood in front of me. He wore well-fitted denim jeans and a red-and-white plaid long-sleeved shirt. He had a white goatee, and thick bundles of black-and-gray dreadlocks hung to his shoulders. Nobility, warmth, and joy emanated from his face.

Then our eyes met, and a warmth exploded within my heart. As we stood there motionless, deep security and peace rippled through me. Empty caverns in my heart filled gently with what radiated out of him. This was not just ascending the mountain. This was soaring above the clouds!

Over the years, I'd wept in moments of fellowship with Jesus. I knew what it was like to have deeply-meaningful friendship with the Holy Spirit, even feeling physical sensations of his love. But I'd never encountered Father God like this. Not this real, intimate, meaningful awareness in the core of my being. Looking into his eyes, I was aware of a thousand emotional vibrations of love and affection, like a symphony penetrating my heart, each sound unique in its expression.

Then I stumbled toward him, toward my Papa, my Father. His arms opened and received me with such tenderness. One moment of his touch, voice, and presence washed away a lifetime of hurt, fear, and pain. Time stood still, at attention to the King of the universe. True joy and deep peace filled my being with a security that was indescribable. My soul echoed in jubilant confidence.

Now things are right! There is nothing that can drag me down from now on. You are my answer, Father. I cannot and will not ever be stopped by fear again!

I finally pulled back, looking up at him. Father God smiled, holding my gaze, then took a few steps back and pointed to the small, yellow dinghy bobbing wildly in the rapids next to him. Behind him, I could hear the thundering roar of the waterfall rushing over the cliff.

"David, let's go on an adventure." His voice was like the sound of water, filled with laughter and love. "Would you come on a ride with me?"

I glanced beyond the yellow dinghy to the turbulent river, dotted with sharp rocks, its violent, tossing waves surging toward the steep drop-off. I hesitated. *Why can't I do this? How can I say no after experiencing such a wonderful presence. What is wrong with me?*

I spotted a large boulder nestled in some bushes to one side. The words stuck in my throat but finally came out. "Can we sit down on that rock instead?" *I can't believe it! I'm saying no to Father God? Why?*

Smiling, Father God agreed. "Let's go."

I staggered over and sat down heavily. The question in my heart stung and finally tumbled out. "Dad, where does this anxiety come from? How can—?"

Silence.

Then Father God wrapped his arms around me, and I felt deep approval penetrate my core again. My shame evaporated. Father God laughed freely, filling my heart with joy to the point that I couldn't hide my own smile. "David, your hesitation isn't the way I made you so it isn't the real you. Let me show you something."

Raising his arm, he pointed far down the river. No bushes and only a few trees lined either bank, so I could see in the distance what looked like a teenager fighting madly to paddle down the river in the yellow dinghy. His brown, unkempt mullet looked familiar, but it was his neon-green sleeveless shirt that tipped me off.

"Dad, is that me?"

Nodding, Father God smiled. "Yes David. That was you. You made me so proud. You still do."

I watched my teenage self helplessly flailing, tossed around in the same small, yellow dinghy in which my Father had invited me to join him. More questions surfaced. "Why was I alone? What does this mean?"

Over the next hour, Father God walked through different forgotten insecurities and anxieties I'd been unaware were holding me captive. Memories from early elementary school of feeling unworthy of attention. Of being misunderstood by a close and trusted friend. Of experiencing the pain of false accusations from a co-worker. Of living with shame and regret over mishandling the ending of a romantic relationship. Allowing fear of taking risks to dominate me because of past painful business failures.

As glimpses and layers of these parts of my life came into view, my faithful Father gently absorbed the devastation and consequences many years of brokenness had accumulated. He healed my heart, answering my questions and restoring clarity about who I really was. As we sat there together on that rock, walking through each tangled chapter of my existence, I saw clearly for the first time in my life how orphan ideas and beliefs had separated me from my heavenly Father.

A potent seed of security and rest was planted inside of me. More than that, my world had been turned upside-down—or rather, right-side-up—by my heavenly Father, who was more real and completely present than I'd ever thought possible. *He's not just in heaven! He's been here inside me all along!*

Opening my eyes, I found myself back in the counselor's office. I looked up at the tall man seated near the door, who had been writing down the descriptions I'd been sharing aloud during our prayer time. Handing me a stack of papers, he exclaimed with wonder, "You really met God in a profound way!"

I felt stunned as I waited in the lobby for Svea to pick me up. There was stillness inside my soul for the first time in my life. I attempted to describe my experience to my wife. Then we retired to bed, and for the first time in months I slept deeply. I awoke early the next morning and went for a walk outside. As I looked out over the distant hills, everything seemed fresh and alive, filling me with a sense of wonder and awe, almost as though I'd been born again.

That day we packed our rental car and drove to the train station. Svea was travelling back to her parents' home where our kids were staying. Dropping her off at the train station, I kissed her goodbye and started on a two-hour drive to meet with a different counselor for further insight and ministry. I was hopeful, yet hesitant. My supernatural encounter with my heavenly Dad had shaken me. Did I even need to meet anyone else for counselling? I felt like a baby, lacking words to express what I was experiencing. Yet I knew there was more.

NEVER-ENDING FLOW

I met the second Christian counselor at a restaurant for coffee. As we sat over our coffee in a booth, he encouraged me that Father God had a deep personal love for me. He urged me to take some time, find some solitude, and put myself in a restful place to receive more of that love.

That was all I needed. Driving back to my hotel, I settled myself into a lawn chair on the second-story balcony outside my room, which offered a vista of brown California hills. Then I waited. Feelings beyond words began welling up in my heart. From the core of my being, I cried out, "Father God, are you this real? If you are, I need more of you!"

I went on, stumbling over my words. "Father, I thought I knew you, but I'm realizing I never have. I want to experience you. Walk with you. I realize I need a dad to carry me. Please help me to have a real relationship with you."

A wave of love and tranquility washed over me. For the next few hours, my Father, our God, communicated his love for me with truthful thoughts and tender emotions. Cradled in the palm of my Creator's hand, I was his, and I knew it. Something in my personhood was being renewed. There was a heavenly security growing inside me I had never known.

The apostle Paul's epistle to the Roman church tells us that as God's children we can call God "Abba," meaning Father (Romans 8:16). In the days that followed, I found that inner cry repeatedly bubbling up in me: "Abba Father, how do you feel about me?" And all over again, I would feel my Father's delight and gentle presence.

> We have a Father God so personally invested in us... that it will take an eternity to fully understand the complexities of his love and affection.

In the weeks and months that would follow, I would return to Scripture and trace Father God's regular intentional involvement in humanity since the Garden of Eden. Despite being a Christian for decades, I was left stunned at the revelation of just who Father God is and how that reflected onto me, his child.

I also began to grasp in a new way the all-consuming, multi-faceted beauty of the Father's nature. He is absolutely gentle (Matthew 11:29). He is completely forgiving (Matthew 23:34). He is altogether comforting (2 Corinthians 1:3). With every millisecond I spend with him, his impact on my being expands. There is no end to the adventure of discovering who he is.

I have become consumed by a conviction that we have a Father God so personally invested in us as his children that it will take an eternity to fully understand the complexities of his love and affection. He completely adores who you are right now. Every day of your existence, he rises from his throne, earnestly seeking for you, longing to connect with your heart wherever you are and whatever you do.

Maybe you've been a Christian your whole life. Maybe you just invited Jesus into your heart. Do you want to know your heavenly Father personally? Have you been living with conscious or unconscious unresolved questions about your life for as long as you can remember? As a believer, do you want more? I'm telling you as one who has discovered that the key to your hope is knowing there is always more! This was certainly true in my story.

As my family and I flew home following this incredible experience, I felt satisfied, hopeful, and at rest with myself. I was more confident I could engage the social cannibalism awaiting me back in my church community. Nothing had changed in my situation except me. Still, as I looked out the airplane window at the flat Manitoba prairies rapidly approaching below, one unsettling question still remained unanswered.

REFLECTIONS

- We were made to experience God as our Father in personal, life-changing ways.

- Father God is real, tangible, loving, and intimately aware of our every need.

QUESTIONS TO CONSIDER

- When challenge or crisis hits your life, what are your deepest questions?

- What does God being your Father mean to you?

- How would you describe your connection with Father God in the last six months?

CONNECTING WITH MY FATHER

May I invite you to join in the following prayer with me.

"Father God, this is it. There is no point in pretending. I need you in a way I've not known you before. I don't completely understand you or myself, but that's okay. All I know is that I want to invite you to meet me. I want to start the adventure of knowing you as my very own Father. Please draw near and show me how personal, immense, and powerful your love is for me. In Jesus's name, amen!"

CHAPTER THREE

Primal Hunger

A couple weeks after my first Father God encounter with the two counselors, that unanswered question began nagging at me. *How could I turn down Father God's invitation to go on a white-water rafting adventure? He created the rapids, rocks, and boat. The safest place for me was with him. What was I thinking?*

And as the daily reality of my soul shifted from insecurity to increased fulfillment, a second question emerged. *Why did it take so long for me to find you, Father God?*

FATHER BLINDNESS

I had been suffering my entire Christian life with what I now call "Father-blindness." This discovery shocked me. Why? Because I had been in love with Jesus since I was twelve years old. I had wonderful, godly, relationally-connected parents. I'd never rebelled against them. I hadn't been abused by my dad. I didn't have any major father issues growing up. Ironically, it was this very warm, connected upbringing that had acted as a barrier to knowing God as my Father, giving me a false sense that I already knew him.

The problem was that I'd been created to need a perfect Father, something no human parent could ever give. Yet how strong my blindness was! With over a decade of full-time ministry experience, I'd even taught on the topic of God as Father. Yet I was blind to the intimate personal connection he wanted with me.

My Father-blindness wasn't because I didn't believe in God as my Father or a member of the Trinity. It didn't mean the gospel lacked power to set me free. Nor did it mean I was limited in my walk with God. What it meant was that I—and perhaps you can identify—was unconsciously and desperately starving to have my primal needs met.

What are primal needs? As I will describe in more detail in the next chapter, primal needs are questions of belonging, provision, protection, and significance. These needs are as persistent and real as physical hunger. Let's take a brief look at each individually.

Belonging is a huge core need for human beings. Social networking platforms like Facebook, Twitter, and Instagram have been adopted by billions of users who log billions of hours each day checking in with their friends, families, and associates around the world. When people lack a sense of belonging and connection, they react in many different ways to meet this core craving. They may binge on sugar and other foods, work harder and longer, over exercise or even engage in self-harm.

Provision is another core need for people anywhere in the world. Whether we are pan-handling for daily sustenance, trying to survive on minimum wage, or inking the next multimillion-dollar deal, we all have basic needs for water, shelter, and food. For those who have accumulated wealth, it may become easy to forget the urgency of this need. But when this need is threatened, we are reminded that without basic provision we can't thrive, let alone survive.

Protection is another core need wired into our biology. Have you felt the adrenaline rush of averting a near certain car accident coming at you while driving? Can you still feel the heart-racing, muscle-aching, sweating physical reaction on the far side of almost getting killed? Whether building high walls around our property, locking doors and windows at night, avoiding a person who doesn't "feel" safe, or constantly looking over our shoulders in fear of being mugged, humans need safety. Consequently, we avoid places, people, or situations where we feel exposed, endangered, or threatened.

Significance is also a core need for people anywhere in the world. When people are younger, they often dream about doing things that make them feel special. As the well-known Russian novelist, Fyodor Dostoyevsky, author of *Crime and Punishment* and *The Brothers Karamazov*, once wrote, "The mystery of human existence lies not in just staying alive, but in finding something to live for."

Whether rich or poor, trying to build our dream business or just survive, we all desire to have a sense of purpose we can feel positive about. A large percentage of memorable movies, novels, and stories involve a protagonist fighting for a cause, principle, or person that in the end, whether they live or die, brings meaning to their lives.

Ultimately, these needs can only be met perfectly by our Father God. In fact, these are the needs a loving father meets in his children. But it is only to the degree that we accept we are our heavenly Dad's children that we will in turn allow him to step into the role of fathering us in our current daily lives.

Bottom line, at a core heart level you and I are still children and always will be no matter how many birthdays we have. Just because we've grown out of potty-training, can tie our own shoelaces, and file our own taxes doesn't mean we ever mature out of having the same needs of a child. As adults, we just become experts at worrying, striving, and pretending our core needs of belonging, provision, protection, or significance have been met.

... we accept we are our heavenly Dad's children...in turn allow him to step into the role of fathering us in our current daily lives.

But I've learned that when I spend even a few moments with my heavenly Dad's heart, those moments transform my state, filling me to overflowing—physically and emotionally—in a way that dramatically affects how I live and relate in my world. Without this living connection, I naturally *react* out of my primal hunger to meet my needs, which in turn leads to a lifestyle of social cannibalism. I grasp and feed on other things, even relationships, to fill these insecure cravings. As we will discuss in the coming chapters, this lifestyle is too often accepted and spiritualized in our churches, even embedded in companies, governments, and national cultural mindsets.

I have encountered this same Father-blindness in many mature, good-willed Christians. Regardless of how long someone has been a believer, what kind of Bible training they have, or how spectacular their ministry experiences have been, something is fatally and fundamentally missing. Often only a crisis or Holy Spirit awakening can peel away the mask of self-confidence and self-protection, revealing eroding insecurities in many different areas of life.

This isn't to point fingers. We all have these areas. Unfortunately, in trying to manage our insecurities and fears, we often rely on cannibalistic behaviors such as gossip, withdrawal, or micro-managing (to name a few) to give us a sense of stability.

Ironically, these very behaviors encourage mindsets that eventually control and manage us. As with my own experiences I've shared, these default mindsets are like seemingly benevolent jail wardens who appear to benefit our lives but are in essence keeping us trapped. As author and Bible teacher Beth Moore writes in her study *Daniel: Lives of Integrity, Words of Prophecy*: "Nothing is more dangerous than friendly captivity."

So where does this blindness come from? It was sin that blinded the human race to who God really is and who we really are. For three years, Jesus modeled an example on earth of what being God's child should look like. Then in three days that encompassed his death, burial, and resurrection, Jesus dealt with the sin obstacle to becoming God's child.

How often I'd readily accepted what Jesus did in those three days as part of my salvation. Yet how rarely I'd stopped to consider what Jesus was modeling in the relationship between himself and our Father during the three years Jesus ministered on Planet Earth. This modeling was recorded in the four New Testament Gospels for our benefit to show us a new way.

As I reread the Gospels over the months following my initial two counselling sessions, my eyes began to open to the stunning dependency Jesus had on his Father for success. Like a small child, I needed to learn this same daily dependency on my heavenly Dad. Because of my past Father-blindness, I'd had no problem relating to Jesus and the Holy Spirit but had little meaningful connection with God as Father.

Nor am I the only one. This blindness is because we don't realize who we really are. We don't know our fundamental identity as God's child. It's interesting that the word "identity" comes from a French word meaning how one regards their own essence. Identity is the lens by which we view ourselves. Could it be that just as a child's relationship with an earthly parent forever influences identity patterns into adulthood, so too a solid relationship with our heavenly Father is our only avenue to establishing in us an eternal, world-changing identity?

WHO'S FEEDING YOUR HUNGER?

Insecurity becomes our personal guide when we regularly try to look to anything or anyone to be for us what only our Father can be. When we live this way, we are spiritually anorexic. This only leads to a vicious cycle of increased insecurity and more attempts of trying to be something we were never intended to be for ourselves. The result is more shame, striving, and anxiety.

> Insecurity becomes our personal guide when we regularly try to look to anything or anyone to be for us what only our heavenly Father can be.

Maybe you've thought or heard someone say: "I don't like hanging around him (or her). He (she) makes me feel insecure." Or how about, "I try to avoid that church . . . restaurant . . . group of people. It brings up insecurity from my past."

Many of us tolerate insecurity as a normal fact of life, not realizing we were never intended to have it as a part of our destiny. The problem is exacerbated when we look to other things, distractions, or people who are not able and never were designed to meaningfully meet our needs. Is it any surprise social cannibalism is a result? Jesus put it like this.

You parents—if your children ask for a loaf of bread, do you give them a stone instead? Or if they ask for a fish, do you give them a snake? Of course not! So if you sinful people know how to give good gifts to your children, how much more will your heavenly Father give good gifts to those who ask him. (Matthew 7:9-11)

Consider the true-life abandonment story of Freddie Friggers. On a cool October night in Quincey, Florida, a newborn baby boy lay naked on a barren floor, its hungry cries splitting the air. With every cry, the baby boy's small arms and feet stiffened, tiny fingers curling into tight fists. Reaching for a blue shawl, his mother wrapped her infant in the frayed, thin cloth. Tears streaked her cheeks, and desperation washed over her. With her drug addiction and life on the streets, she couldn't care for a newborn, but what to do with her son?

Pulling the blue bundle to her chest, she headed out into the cold night to a small recreation park nearby. Under a brisk breeze, a renewed shrill came from the baby. Was there some sheltered space she could leave him? The baby quieted as the new mother clutched him close, crossing the street to a dark alley. Frantic eyes spotted a weathered blue dumpster in the shadows. Approaching the bin, she found a tipped cardboard box full of newspaper. *This should do!*

Her infant son lay quietly in her arms now, fast asleep. The mother looked at the helpless, chubby face one last time. Before she could change her mind, she quickly nestled the blue bundle in the cardboard box. Tucking the sports section of the paper over him like a crumpled black-and-white blanket, she lowered the dumpster lid into place and disappeared into the night.

I have dramatized this real-life story to make a point. If undiscovered, how long can a newborn live, abandoned to a cold night in that cardboard box? Ten hours? Twenty-four hours? Forty-eight?

Let's face it! Without regular nurturing of his primal needs, this infant would be doomed because he is completely helpless and totally needy. In the same way, you as a believer are an infant in Christ desperately *needing* an active, healthy relationship with your Father to thrive. Without that relationship, you too will scream, starve, thrash around and die of exposure.

The beautiful ending to this true-life story is that Freddie Friggers was discovered in time and within two months was adopted by a loving elderly couple. As his needs were actively met by his adoptive parents, he developed into a successful inventor, multi-millionaire businessman, and in time a loving husband and father himself.

What about you? How central is Father God to your daily existence. Is it like that of a needy, helpless toddler to a loving parent? The above anecdote highlights the importance of choosing and seeing Father God as our center for life. This is not a theological decision. This requires living with a correct view of ourselves.

Our primary identity determines everything we say and do. It becomes our reference point for how to make every decision, deal with every crisis, and respond in every relationship. Because our primary identity is foundational to our existence, it determines:

- The type of resources we draw from.

- How we feel about ourselves and others in conflict and struggle.

- What kind of meaning we experience in life.

What is your primary view of yourself? A businessman? Pastor? Father? Mother? Wife? Husband? Christian? What do you work toward or look to for creating security in areas of provision, belonging, protection, and significance? We have been called to follow and imitate Christ's example, as the apostle Peter reminds us.

> For God called you to do good, even if it means suffering, just as Christ suffered for you. He is your example, and you must follow in his steps. (I Peter 2:21)

So if we're called to follow Christ, wouldn't it make sense to learn what Jesus's foundational core view of himself was?

JESUS'S CORE IDENTITY

According to the Gospel accounts, Jesus referred to himself as God (John 20:28-29), Son of Man (Matthew 20:28), Savior (Matthew 26:28), Life (John 4:14). But more than anything else, Jesus referred to himself directly and indirectly as God's Son. His number-one reference for himself, his life, and activity was his Father.

Consider the many times Jesus referred to his Father throughout the Gospels. Jesus believed in his Father's love for him (John 5:20). Jesus received authority from his Father (John 5:22, 27). Jesus lived to fulfill his Father's mission (Luke 22:42). Jesus taught his disciples how to pray by addressing their Father in heaven (Matthew 6:9-13). Jesus made it clear he could do nothing by himself, only what he saw his Father doing (John 5:19). His last prayer the night before his torturous crucifixion was to his Father (John 17). As you follow the life of Jesus, you cannot help but realize his core identity was anchored in who he was to his Father.

So if Jesus's core identity as God and Lord was a Son, how much more should you and I carry the same as our foundational identity? Do we think we can fulfill our eternal destiny a different way? Jesus highlighted this point when speaking to his disciples.

> He called a little child to him, and placed the child among them. And he said: "Truly I tell you, unless you change and become like little children, you will never enter the kingdom of heaven. Therefore, whoever takes the lowly position of this child is the greatest in the kingdom of heaven.
> (Matthew 18:2-4, NIV)

What child-like qualities was Jesus referencing? I'm sure an obvious application might be the need for us to be humble. This is true, but why? Simply put, humility is necessary because as actual children we are in constant state of neediness. Yes, you read that right—neediness.

So am I saying that Jesus wants us to become needy? The truth is that we already are. Learning to become like a child means learning to be aware of our needs and letting our heavenly Father meet our needs as any earthly father would. The difference being that our heavenly Dad can meet those needs perfectly.

REFLECTIONS

- We are "Father-blind" when we seek to live our Christian lives without a living dependency on God as Father for every area of our lives.

- Just like Jesus, our foundational identity should be that we are God's son or daughter.

QUESTIONS TO CONSIDER

- Where would you put yourself between the following two extremes? 1) I had a great dad, so I already know what Father God is like; 2) I had a horrible, abusive father on earth, so I cannot imagine connecting with a heavenly Father. How does your past influence your chosen daily relational habits toward God as an active, loving Father?

- Which way of seeing yourself do you think about or talk about the most? I.e., as mother, business owner, Christian, funny, hard-working, etc.

CONNECTING WITH MY FATHER

May I invite you to join in the following prayer with me.

"Father God, I am seeing more than ever that I am your son/daughter before anything else. Help me to grow and accept this reality as my foundational reality. I confess there are times and places I've leaned on my own abilities. I want to live with the same relational flow Jesus had with you as Father when he was on the earth. Help me to remember when I feel stressed, angry, or down to run to you as the perfect answer for all of my questions, challenges, and desires. In Jesus's name, amen!"

CHAPTER FOUR

The Four Needs Of A Child

*D*oes all that seem confusing or overly complicated? It's actually simple. As I stated earlier, just like earthly kids, you and I were created with four core needs that can only be met by our heavenly Father.

And it makes total sense that our Father God can meet them perfectly because he is the one who created us with those needs. You'd think I was pretty foolish if I claimed that only my favorite drill gun, a French poodle, or my GMC 4X4 truck could satisfy the fundamental needs of my two-year-old daughter. As her father, I am obviously the best source for meeting my own daughter's needs.

Likewise, when we experience our heavenly Dad meeting us in our needs and deepest insecurities, this anchors us, reminding us of who we really are—God's child. In my own life, I have discovered that when I live solely as my heavenly Dad's child, all other identities fall into their rightful place. In consequence, I walk with a stability, clarity, and hope no other identity can give me.

In the last chapter, we discussed briefly that the four core universal needs we all carry are provision, belonging, protection, and significance. Each one of these needs is foundational to a child's development. How these needs are met and by whom greatly influence how a child will see themself.

> when I live solely as my heavenly Dad's child, all other identities fall into their rightful place.

It is for this reason I call these four needs Identity Molders. Why? Because what we believe about these core needs and how we go about trying to meet each need plays a major role in how we see ourselves. Which in turn determines just what we accept about our identity. Once again, let's take a closer look at each of these core needs individually in terms of being Identity Molders.

PROVISION IDENTITY MOLDER

The Gospel of Matthew gives an account of Satan tempting Jesus in the desert before he began his public ministry (Matthew 4:2-11). Why this time and place? Let's go back to Jesus at thirty years of age taking a solitary trek into an arid mountainous desert with daytime temperatures hovering around a hundred degrees Fahrenheit. Wild animals, dangerous snakes and scorpions, and unlawful bandits lurk in dark shadows.

Satan has one good chance to take out the Son of God before Jesus starts his rescue mission to humanity. How better to stop Jesus than by questioning his identity as a Son by tempting him to meet his own core needs apart from his Father? The Son is alone in this dangerous desert. He is weak and tired from fasting for forty days.

He doesn't yet have a list of amazing accomplishments or a huge following, so his confidence shouldn't be that unshakable. It's a perfect chance to take him out, right?

Wrong! Let's take a look at Satan's first try.

> After fasting forty days and forty nights, he [Jesus] was hungry. The tempter [Satan] came to him and said, "If you are the Son of God, tell these stones to become bread." Jesus answered, "It is written: 'Man shall not live on bread alone, but on every word that comes from the mouth of God.'" (Matthew 4:2-4, NIV)

In round one, Satan challenges Jesus's position as a Son by daring him to take care of his own needs. Jesus stands on Scripture, pointing to the true source of provision—the mouth of God.

Provision is a powerful identity molder. From the moment we are born, we have provision needs. Babies scream for milk. Children listen to the quiet chatter of their parents on payday. Teenagers whine for allowance. Young adults pay a fortune for an education in the hopes that it pays well in the form of a good job. Adults develop ulcers and/or struggle with depression and addictions out of fear of losing their jobs. Even as Christians, when we visit a new church, we inspect the bulletin, analyze different programs, listen to the preaching, all to determine whether this church will provide for our spiritual needs.

Our world builds multi-billion-dollar industries targeting provision insecurities. And of course, we all have material, spiritual, and social needs that require provision. But if our existence is rooted as

God's son or daughter, our reflexive response will be, "Father, I need you. Only you can meet this need."

Jesus addressed this issue in his well-known Sermon on the Mount.

> Look at the birds. They don't plant or harvest or store food in barns, for your heavenly Father feeds them. And aren't you far more valuable to him than they are? Can all your worries add a single moment to your life? . . . For the pagans run after all these things, and your heavenly Father knows that you need them. (Matthew 6:26-27, 32)

Did you get what Jesus is saying here? Your Father knows what you need! He is your perfect provider. Will you trust him?

Our core questions as human beings regarding provision include the following.

- Will my physical needs be provided for now and/or when I'm too old to work?

- Who will provide for my social and emotional needs?

- Will this church/group/community provide for my family's spiritual needs?

But the real question we should be asking is how secure you are in the knowledge that God already knows all your needs, and as a loving Father, wants to provide them for you, as Jesus also declared in his Sermon on the Mount.

So do not worry, saying, 'What shall we eat?' or 'What shall we drink?' or 'What shall we wear?' For the pagans run after all these things, and your heavenly Father knows that you need them. But seek first his kingdom and his righteousness, and all these things will be given to you as well. (Matthew 6:31-33, NIV)

BELONGING IDENTITY MOLDER

The second way Satan challenged Jesus's identity as a Son was by tempting him to test his Father's loyalty.

Then the devil took him to the holy city, Jerusalem, to the highest point of the Temple, and said, "If you are the Son of God, jump off! For the Scriptures say, 'He will order his angels to protect you . . .'" (Matthew 4:5-6a)

This is the only temptation where Satan refers to Jesus's relationship with his Father, questioning the strength of their bond. In other words, "If you are the Son of God, prove it! If you really do belong to God, he will help you out."

Our need to belong is powerful. Regardless of what people may claim, we *all* have the need to belong. God stated when he created Adam and Eve, "It is not good for man to be alone" (Genesis 2:18). Research shows that socially connected people tend to live longer, seemingly shielded from a range of conditions such as heart disease and cancer. Research also shows that heartbreak or being rejected in some way can actually reduce our ability to think, suppressing our IQ.

The truth is that most decisions we make relate to belonging. Our brains scan our environment several times a second, looking for clues in body posture, eye pupil dilation, and tone of voice. *Are these people friendly? Do they like me? Can I count on them in the future?* This scientific reality means that belonging is a major preoccupation for the human race.

Jesus let his Father meet these needs. On more than one occasion, Father God publicly declared that Jesus was his Beloved Son (Matthew 3:17; 17:5; Mark 1:11; 9:7; 2 Peter 1:17), including at his baptism, then later at his transfiguration when he appeared on the mountain with Moses and Elijah (Matthew 17:1–8; Mark 9:2–8; Luke 9:28–36). When Jesus prayed his final prayer of blessing over his disciples before heading to the Garden of Gethsemane, he described his Father's love for him as being eternal before the worlds were created.

> . . . the glory you gave me because you loved me even before the world began! (John 17:24).

There is no question that Jesus demonstrated an uncommon security grounded in his Father's love. Our own core questions as humans regarding belonging include the following.

- Am I loved, accepted, affirmed, and/or appreciated?

- Do people enjoy or delight in me?

- Am I valuable to someone?

The real question should be this. Will you allow your Father into your life? He is standing at your door right now, calling your name and knocking (Revelation 3:20). If you let him in, you'll enjoy a feast together of heavenly proportions.

PROTECTION IDENTITY MOLDER

In his third round of attack, Satan piggybacks off his last challenge regarding Jesus's view of himself, this time tempting Jesus to test his Father's protection. Jesus once again stands on God's Word, affirming that a Son doesn't need or want to put their Father to the test.

> Then the devil took him to the holy city, Jerusalem, to the highest point of the Temple, and said, "If you are the Son of God, jump off! For the Scriptures say, 'He will order his angels to protect you. And they will hold you up with their hands so you won't even hurt your foot on a stone.'" Jesus responded, "The Scriptures also say, 'You must not test the LORD YOUR GOD.'" (Matthew 4:5-7)

Feeling exposed and vulnerable is a trauma that can leave a mark long after the actual incident. Years ago, I ministered with an elderly woman who shared her story with me. As a teenager, she'd been abducted at her high school by a man with a shotgun. Though the police were able to apprehend the man before he could take her off school property, the damage was done. The woman suffered nightmares for decades. Even though she'd been to Bible School, had a loving husband, children, and was co-pastoring a church, she still felt vulnerable, exposed, and terrified.

Thankfully, many years after that traumatic event, Father God brought freedom to this precious woman. Regardless of how much time or achievement we may have behind us, we need his perfect protection more than anything else. The world sends us regular messages reminding us of the constant social, financial, and physical dangers all around us. Yet as children, we were never designed to protect ourselves.

Jesus knew this when he prayed for his disciples, present and future, at the end of the Last Supper before he headed to the Garden of Gethsemane.

> Holy Father . . . you have given me your name; now protect them by the power of your name . . . (John 17:11).

When Jesus taught his disciples to pray to the Father in the Lord's prayer, he included, "deliver us from evil" (Matthew 6:13). The Old Testament book of Proverbs also reminds us of our Father's protection.

> The LORD WILL BE YOUR CONFIDENCE, FIRM AND STRONG, AND WILL KEEP YOUR FOOT FROM BEING CAUGHT IN A TRAP. (Proverbs 3:26, AMP)

Or as The New Living Translation phrases this same passage:

> You can go to bed without fear; you will lie down and sleep soundly. You need not be afraid of sudden disaster... for the LORD IS YOUR SECURITY. HE WILL KEEP YOUR FOOT FROM BEING CAUGHT IN A TRAP. (Proverbs 3:24-26)

The core questions we ask ourselves regarding protection include the following.

- Am I safe, covered, and secure here?

- Is it okay to relax and be myself here?

Do you know what it feels like to be at ease in every situation, relationship, and challenge you encounter? For many of us, uneasiness is so a part of our life that we've forgotten what it's like to be carefree like a child. But when we invite Father God to be our protection, we live in incredible peace and security. In this place, you can truly discover who you were created to be. Walking with his safety and security, you can afford to take risks, explore, and learn what your Father has invested in you.

SIGNIFICANCE IDENTITY MOLDER

In the final round, Satan attempts to knock out Jesus by tempting him to create significance, purpose, and meaning for himself outside of who he really was. Again, Jesus stands on the truth of God's Word and his identity as his Father's Son instead of engaging Satan's offered shortcut.

> Next the devil took him to the peak of a very high mountain and showed him all the kingdoms of the world and their glory. "I will give it all to you," he said, "if you will kneel down and worship me."
>
> "Get out of here, Satan," Jesus told him. "For the Scriptures say, 'You must worship the LORD YOUR GOD AND SERVE ONLY HIM.'" (Matthew 4:8-10)

In our own lives, this temptation invites us to a short-cut of building our identity around ourselves, a talent, a person, or a title to find purpose or meaning. Any attempt to build personal significance outside of our loving Father's embrace leads us to bow down and worship something other than God, leaving us empty, toiling, and alone. Consider the parable Jesus told of the prodigal son, who sought to find his sense of meaning beyond his father in a different land (Luke 15:11-32). It didn't work! Only when he repented, returned to his father, and took his place again as his father's son did he find true significance.

personal significance outside of our loving Father's embrace leads us to worship something other than God, leaving us empty, toiling, and alone.

In contrast, as Son of God, Jesus knew from day one that his significance, meaning, and purpose came solely from his Father. Just look at the first recorded human words Jesus ever uttered when he was just twelve years old. The overall context was when his earthly parents, Mary and Joseph, had taken Jesus to Jerusalem to celebrate Passover at the temple (Luke 2:41-52). After being separated for three days, his parents finally found Jesus at the temple. When they asked Jesus where he'd been, his answer made clear he knew the source of his significance.

> "But why did you need to search?" he asked. "Didn't you know that I must be in my Father's house?" (Luke 2:49)

From early on, Jesus knew he was God's Son. With child-like humility, he obeyed his Father in everything. Both his sense of purpose and meaning for his existence came from his heavenly Dad. Jesus lived in such a way as to absolutely need his Father's view and definition for his life, as he explained to his disciples.

> "My food," said Jesus, "is to do the will of him who sent me and to finish his work." (John 4:34, NIV)

On one of my sleepovers as a teenager, my friend Bryan and I decided to see how much junk food we could eat. We packed our stomachs with bags of chips, pop, and chocolate until late at night. But the next morning, our reckoning came as we found ourselves sitting nauseated on the toilet. I learned my lesson that it is impossible to thrive on junk food alone. In contrast, healthy food benefits us by giving us energy, nourishment, enjoyment, and life.

Just as nutritious food is necessary for us to function, we have an internal need to receive our Father's purpose and definition. Deriving our primary significance from anything other than our heavenly Dad's definition for us is like ingesting stale, preprocessed, nutrient-less, chemically-injected junk food. It may taste good for a moment, but in time we will lose energy, focus, and passion for life.

"Junk-food" life plans include making well-intentioned plans for your own future or for those you love. For years, people around me had definitions, ideas, and plans for my life based on how they saw me as the son and logical successor of my father. I couldn't help hearing and being influenced by so many well-intentioned voices. In the small prairie town where I grew up, everyone knew everyone and felt comfortable speaking into each other's lives. Several businessmen I respected regularly encouraged me to leave salaried pastoring and serve God by starting a business. Friends and relatives proudly declared I was called to life-long ministry commitments. Still others I held in high regard strongly recommended I get my degree to build a career in academia.

Over time a heavy weight of deep insecurity grew about my purpose. In the end, I realized I couldn't feed my God-given need for significance with the "junk food" others were offering. I had to receive significance and purpose from my heavenly Dad.

Now I love hanging out with Father God, learning about my life's calling and how to use my gifts for him. It is such an incredible experience to have your heavenly Dad, Creator of the cosmos, share his plans with you. Having your purpose defined by him is such a deeply satisfying way to live. And it is so blessedly restful not to strive for significance but just allow your Father to explain how your gifts and personality work for a greater purpose.

The core questions we struggle with regarding significance include the following.

- Does my life have meaning?

- What is my purpose?

- Is there a reason for my existence?

These are great questions that we will typically ask throughout our lives. But the real question is this. From whom are we seeking to find our answers?

I am so excited because you are on the verge of great adventures. Your heavenly Dad has been waiting for an eternity to meet your deepest needs with himself. You are his child. It is your primary identity, and only he can satisfy!

REFLECTIONS

- Humanity's core needs are provision, belonging, protection, and significance.

- Jesus was our perfect example of how to live and overcome from an identity molded by relationship with Father God as our absolute source for all our needs.

QUESTIONS TO CONSIDER

- What habits of thought and action do you apply to each of your four core needs in a typical week?

- What comes up for you when considering how Jesus lived his life as God's Son?

CONNECTING WITH MY FATHER

May I invite you to join in the following prayer with me.

"Father God, I desire to follow the example of your Son Jesus in living as your child on Earth. For this reason, I want to stop trying to meet my needs on my own terms. I want to rely on you as my Father for all my needs for provision, belonging, protection, and significance. I invite you to show me who you are in these areas. Thank you for always being present and available to meet me. I only want your help. In Jesus's name, amen!"

CHAPTER FIVE

Hunger Pangs

I love eating, whether it be sweet, rich desserts or salty, savory finger foods. I try to eat regular, responsible portions of nutritious food. But when unexpected life demands force me to skip a couple meals, the ravages of hunger begin screaming my need for sustenance. My stomach starts growling, and my brain slows down. As weakness sets in, I can become a grumpy bear. In this state, it is easy to shift my standards for eating healthy salad greens to donuts and Doritos.

Perhaps you can relate. It is no accident God created us with four core needs natural to all children—provision, protection, belonging, and significance. Throughout our lives, these needs are as persistent and real to our sense of survival as the physical hunger burning in our stomachs.

Our Father God's heart longs to meet every one of our needs. As our perfect heavenly Dad, he perfectly parents us, satisfying all our needs. But if we choose to live a life that creates our own solutions and finds satisfaction for our needs in other places, our hunger will never be satisfied. It is like fighting for maggot-and-dung-infested hay-feed when a multi-course meal of rare meats, cheeses, salads, spicy treats, and sweet delights is waiting to be served.

What is the result of trying to satisfy our core hunger without letting Father God meet our needs as any good dad would? Insecurity. Insecurity is like the flashing red light on the dashboard of our minds and hearts, alerting us that our primal needs are depleted and that we need our heavenly Father to fill our "tank."

And just like a small child needs parental care throughout the day, we need regular connection with our Father. Without this connection, insecurity grows, becoming an earthly reality we must deal with. You and I were not designed to live in a constant state of insecurity. As I will explain in the next chapter, we were originally created for Eden's gardens and to enjoy a perfect Father's presence.

Insecurity screams at us, "Meet my needs!" As our anxiety level rises, its messages clamor: "Could I fail at this job? . . . I'm a terrible mother! . . . I'm ruining my children! . . . How am I going to pay our bills next month? . . . What's going to happen if this project is done wrong? . . . There's something wrong with me! . . . Why can't I drop these pounds? . . . What will my wife think of me?"

As soon as you encounter feelings of insecurity, your body's endocrine and nervous system alerts you. Your mind and heart desperately seek out ways to break free from insecurity. Truly, insecurity is torment to the human soul. And this is where social cannibalism emerges.

Some may say insecurity is a normal part of life and offers a chance to grow. And of course, there are outwardly-confident people who claim they are not insecure. Some people even equate security with confidence. But in truth, the two are very different. Confidence is being aware of my own gifts and talents and believing I can use these to manage any challenges surrounding me. When I was a pastor, I lived with confidence until the circumstances confronting me were well beyond my gifts and talents. Then my confidence slipped into crisis.

In contrast, while I'd known what it meant to be confident, I didn't know deep security until I encountered it through a Father-centered lifestyle where all my needs were met. Unlike confidence, this security is immovable because it is based in something eternal, far bigger than us. The messages radiating from this kind of security assure me: "Because I love you, you are worthy! . . . Because I made you, you already are beautiful! . . . Because I am with you, you are able to overcome."

Whether we find ourselves on a path of quality relationships and job success or, conversely, on a path of self-harm and conflict with others, our whole being is oriented to crave security. There may be times where our hunger for financial provision seems to have been satiated by business or career success. Such earthly wins might boost our confidence in our financial status. But if our daily feeding isn't coming from our heavenly Dad, any unexpected economic downturn, layoff, or illness can steal our sense of confidence.

If we don't rely relationally on God as our Father, we are left starving for provision, protection, belonging, and significance and with only ourselves to satisfy those. Some of us may be starving with a particular unmet need. Others may be choking on scraps to feed several needs. Still others of us may be guarding our secret solution to a particular need.

Whatever the case, many of us do not perceive our own insecurity until crisis in a relationship, work, or political environment threatens our food supply. As the urgency of the situation grows, it gradually threatens our well-being and peace. Eventually, insecurity increases to full-blown panic as the reality of an unmet need hits home. Just as a starving person scarfs down the nearest edible thing, we end up cannibalizing ourselves or others in a desperate attempt to avoid the pain of security starvation.

> Just as a starving person scarfs down the nearest edible thing, we end up cannibalizing ourselves or others in a desperate attempt to avoid the pain of security starvation.

Cannibalism can take many faces. It may be micro-managing our spouse's behaviour in public. Or trolling Facebook for likes and approval while filling up with self-loathing. It may be bingeing on ESPN. Or online shopping to avoid unresolved resentment. Or silencing our voice to gain love or approval. Our natural inclinations to avoid, control, hoard, or comply to cope during a crisis will only lead us in a relentless, self-perpetuating cycle of insecurity. The personal cost is high as such cannibalistic behavior eats away at our God-given potential.

Our world is polluted with insecurity. Anxiety, depression, shame, polarization, dishonor, and judgment have become normal. These disorders are reported in our news, grafted into our political and economic systems, and intertwined in our expectations of the future. As a part of God's family, you have been designed to be the hospitable host of our Father's banquet table of love (Psalm 23:5), feeding friends, relatives, co-workers, and neighbors who are starving in insecurity. But how can you save anyone else if you are starving yourself? Such was the case for me.

SHIFTING SHADOWS

After my return from the California trip where I encountered God as my Father, I was hungry to explore this new relationship. In the absence of a strong, well-respected senior pastor, our church continued to struggle with conflicts and misunderstandings as our team of elders and church founders tried to find a way forward. Congregants were leaving as people became disillusioned by the lack of direction and clarity.

Since I was still serving as interim associate pastor, there were many opinions about what I should do. Some felt I was missing God's calling by not stepping into the senior pastoral role. Some were gossiping that I had an agenda to subvert the leadership team for my own ambitions. On one occasion, I was out walking when I spotted a respected ministry leader. When I called out a greeting, he immediately crossed the road to avoid speaking to me.

> Just like a toddler needs to experience daily a present reality of an earthly father, gentle protector, and provider, so I too was made to daily need and experience my heavenly Dad.

It was deeply painful to see even good people leave the church with a distorted view of my motivations and struggles. Yet despite the difficulties, I was actually seeing shifts in myself during this time from anxiety to security. As I began to understand that my deep needs were forever and always meant to be met by my heavenly Father, I learned a new rhythm of coming to him for everyday life challenges. Just like a toddler needs to experience daily a present reality of an earthly father, gentle protector, and provider, so, I, too was made to daily need and experience my heavenly Dad. His loving smile on my heart each morning brought physical, emotional, and spiritual calm to my whole being.

The consequences of this new rhythm were gradual but dramatic. People close to me began asking what had happened to me. Walking into leadership or congregational meetings that had previously felt threatening no longer caused me anxiety. I was able to confront conflict without being defensive or anxious. Suddenly, what were once big questions about my future or how provision needs would be met drifted out of consciousness.

In so many ways, like a toddler learning to walk for the first time, I felt I was learning a new way I had never known. I was alive again, safe, care-free, and full of wonder. As I grew in knowing my Father more deeply, I began seeing and understanding myself more fully. It was around this time that I started understanding patterns of social cannibalism in relationships, organizations, and throughout history. This confirmed to me my growing conviction that only a loving Father could help a world of spiritual orphans caught in self-destruction.

REFLECTIONS

- When our primal needs are not being met by Father God, insecurity grows and dominates our perceptions, desires, decisions, and beliefs.

- Cannibalizing ourselves or others arises from the pain of avoiding security starvation.

QUESTIONS TO CONSIDER

- In which areas in your life would you be tempted to misperceive the confidence you have carried for a deeper security arising from knowing God as Father?

- How do you see your relationship or lack of relationship with God as your Dad affecting you?

CONNECTING WITH MY FATHER

May I invite you to join in the following prayer with me.

"Father God, I am so grateful that you care perfectly and constantly for my well-being at every possible level. Please show me areas I have felt and lived self-sufficiently from you. And please forgive me for those parts of my life where I haven't invited you to be my Dad. Like an infant, help me see and relate to you as the center of all my daily needs. You are my security and hope in the biggest and smallest parts of my life. In Jesus's name, amen!"

CHAPTER SIX

Out From The Shadows

*W*hile finishing my last year of college, I got a part-time job at a youth crisis center to help pay for tuition expenses. The center offered overnight housing and support for youth twelve to seventeen years of age caught in a government-run foster care system. Many of those staying at the home had no parents, and most had no relatives who could support them.

It was my first evening shift working as a home supervisor when I learned how easily social cannibalism can erupt. In the center of a throng of boys, one teen's white-knuckled fists were raised over another youth. His eyes twitched erratically, his breath coming in gasps, as he shouted furiously, "Do you want me to kill you? Do you?"

Anger and hatred sliced the atmosphere like razors as the group tensed for a response. Trying to jerk himself free, the other teen sneered vindictively, "Go ahead. Do it! Are you afraid? Do it! Come on, hit me!"

Shrieks broke out as the two erupted into violence, rolling, kicking, punching, even scratching at each other wildly. Blood splattered onto a nearby wall. The gang of watching boys cheered them on in frenzied jubilation. When we saw a chance, another youth worker and I stepped in, separating the two bloodied teens.

I quickly learned that these boys lived by a different and dangerous sets of rules. Without parents and abandoned by the system, they'd been left to fend for themselves. In trying to connect with them, I discovered that these precious young people were trapped in a state of constant suspicion, anger, sadness, anxiety, and loneliness. Because of this, they were unable to form healthy, emotionally stable connections with adults, their closest friends, and even themselves. Their bedtime routine involved a weapons check for each room. The creativity of homemade knives, bombs, and firearms alerted me that something was very wrong. The devastation of trauma had birthed social cannibalism among the most vulnerable in our society.

In technical terms, an orphan is a person, whether child or adult, who has lost both parents due to death. Unfortunately, our world is full of "social" orphans. These are people whose parents abandoned them as children, abused them throughout their growing-up years, or simply lived emotionally and socially withdrawn from their children. Scientific research demonstrates that most social orphans suffer a variety of common behaviours and emotional challenges throughout their lives. They may struggle with unconscious anxiety about being abandoned or acute internal and external restlessness.

In consequence, their brain's internal fight or flight response is constantly on alert even in safe environments. This causes many such "orphans," whether foster kids, social orphans, or even those adopted from difficult circumstances into stable, loving homes, to struggle with a defensive view of the world, making it difficult to be flexible and trusting. Compounding the situation are feelings of anger, panic, helplessness, and sorrow that distort their perceptions and beliefs in many of life's situations. Many also struggle with a sense of being unworthy, flawed, and undeserving. Can you imagine trying to live a happy life while constantly struggling with these feelings and perceptions brewing under the surface?

So, what is going on here? Over the years, research, documentaries, and news reports have fostered a greater understanding of the trauma a child experiences when tragically separated from or abused by their biological parents. The word *trauma* comes from a Greek word meaning *to wound*. In this context, it refers to the mental and emotional wounds caused by shocking events or experiences. Such trauma negatively affects the brain and consequently a person's ability to function in a healthy way.

One consequence of trauma that has become more publicized is post-traumatic stress disorder (PTSD). This is frequently experienced by soldiers who have faced major violence and trauma in war zones. Many of these soldiers return to their families and friends with mental and emotional challenges. In past centuries, PTSD and other such mental illnesses were often dismissed as "just in your head." But we now know that these mental and emotional wounds actually damage brain chemistry and wiring.

Another type of brain-altering trauma occurs when infants and children are separated from their parents. Many times, these painful emotions of abandonment and rejection occur before conscious memory is formed. Whether the separation was due to death of parents, poverty, neglect, a dysfunctional home, or actual abuse, separation trauma can follow these children into adulthood. Many develop negative coping mechanisms to manage feelings of worthlessness, anger, panic, helplessness, and sorrow. Such behaviors can include physically or emotionally aggressive behavior, stealing, impulsive decision-making, complete social withdrawal, compulsive lying, drug and/or alcohol abuse to name a few. Many social science studies show these painful patterns.

For many adopted and foster children, these emotions and behaviors come from being trapped by their brain's brokenness, causing them to integrate wrong messages about how they see themselves. Years ago, close friends of mine confided in me the painful struggles of parenting their adopted child. They had raised three well-adjusted biological children of their own. But these same parenting approaches had seemingly failed with their adopted child.

Their adopted son had been placed in foster care after years of physical and emotional abuse and neglect under the care of his biological mother, who was living with a drug addiction. They'd adopted him when he was seven years old. From the first day, their entire family had fallen in love with his dimple-faced smile, blond hair, and easy-going, likeable personality. But by his teenage years, my friends became alarmed at their son's self-destructive behaviors. Despite a loving, supportive, and structured environment, he began stealing and bold-faced lying.

At one point, their adopted son was caught stealing money from the family's vacation jar. On another occasion, a shotgun was found stashed beneath his bed. Horrified and saddened, my friends reached out for help. Sadly, they found that their experiences were not the exception but more common for social orphans. Their son's early childhood traumatic experiences had disrupted his brain's development, causing him to be hypervigilant, impulsive, and distrustful of others who loved him.

You might ask me, "David, why are we talking about this? What does this have to do with my relationship with God as my Father."

I am talking about this because I am describing you! And myself, of course. You and I have been directly and indirectly impacted by separation trauma in our relationship with our heavenly Father. Let me explain. Whether or not you've been abandoned by earthly parents, you were born into this world separated from your true parent, our heavenly Dad. And just as any child needs constant, healthy connection with a parent to develop emotionally, mentally, and physically, we need ongoing connection with our heavenly Father to grow secure and live with healthy, heavenly responses in every area of our lives.

Research into brain development reveals that infants can recognize their mother's scent and sense their mother's emotions. Both proximity and scent bring calm to a child. So when infants are separated from their biological parents, they go into shock. This causes their tiny bodies to secrete stress hormones while also reducing the production of helpful neurochemicals in the brain. The result is impaired development of that part of the brain responsible for social bonding, decision-making, and impulse control. While there is hope with the sacrificial support of faith-filled adoptive/foster parents, the journey can be long and difficult. The same reality of shock and trauma caused by separation between mother and child is/has been evident in our relationship with God as our Father.

So how exactly has separation from our Father God traumatized the human race, consequently creating one big, global orphanage? Father God created the first humans, Adam and Eve, and placed them in a beautiful garden (Genesis 2:8-15). Scripture tells us that God walked with them in the cool of the day (Genesis 3:8). They enjoyed connection and relationship with God as their Father.

Tragically, on one particular day, sin interrupted Father God's custom of walking with his children when Adam and Eve disobeyed by eating from the tree of the knowledge of good and evil, whose fruit God had commanded them not to eat (Genesis 2:16-17; 3:6-7). Once released in the world, sin contaminated everything, including Adam and Eve's personhood, separating them and their future offspring (you and I) from knowing God as an intimate, present, tangible Father.

Sin also introduced shame to Adam and Eve, compelling them to want to cover up their nakedness (Genesis 3:7). Shame separated them further from their heavenly Dad by cursing their identity as God's children, whispering lies that they were worthless. This separation from Father God meant that Adam and Eve and all of humanity since have lived like social orphans, devastated by the trauma of being separated from their heavenly Dad. That separation trauma resulted in humanity living with deep insecurities, anxieties, unworthiness, anger, sorrow, and shame never intended by Father God for his children.

As social and spiritual orphans separated from God, no one on earth had the power to live sinlessly, therefore knowing God as Father was impossible (Romans 3:20; Hebrews 10:1). But God had a plan to nullify sin and its contaminating effects on humanity, culminating in Jesus, God's perfect reflection of who God is as our Father and friend (Isaiah 9:6; John 14:7-9). The Gospel accounts of Matthew, Mark, Luke, and John testify to Jesus, born fully God and fully human into Jewish Palestine (John 1:14).

As we saw earlier, the Son of God was tempted by Satan but lived a perfect life by maintaining a connected relational reliance on his Father (John 5:30). After three years of public ministry, Jesus neutralized sin's contamination by offering himself as a perfect sacrifice for sin (John 10:18). Through his death, burial, and resurrection, we have been restored to our position as God's sons and daughters. We once again have perfect access to God as our Father (1 John 3:1) and we are invited to a new reality of actively and personally relating to God as our Father (Romans 8:15).

Though God never stopped being a Father to humanity, the human race lost its ability to know him because of sin's barrier. The Old Testament contains many stories of spiritually orphaned individuals who knew God but had little to no personal knowledge of him as a Father. In fact, in over four thousand years of recorded Old Testament biblical history, God is directly referenced as Father only nineteen times. In one of the most revealing passages, Father God expresses his fatherly yearning to the nation of Israel through the prophet Jeremiah.

> I would love to treat you as my own children! I wanted nothing more than to give you this beautiful land—the finest possession in the world. I looked forward to your calling me 'Father,' (Jeremiah 3:19)

Extrabiblical Jewish writings and oral tradition (Talmud and Mishna) do mention God as Father. But their basis for a relationship with God was only through perfectly keeping the Old Testament law. This was and still is impossible. For this reason, it was necessary for God's Son, Jesus Christ, to come as the perfect sacrifice and only way by which human beings can be restored to relationship with God, as Jesus himself makes clear:

> I am the way, the truth, and the life. No one can come to the Father except through me. (John 14:6)

Jesus became "the way" by perfectly fulfilling/keeping God's law as given to Moses on Mount Sinai (Exodus 19-24). By believing in Jesus, we automatically enter into the same connection and relational experience Jesus has with his Father. This means that whatever your earthly father was like—abusive, absent-minded, strict, or gentle and kind—it doesn't matter. You are connected to Father God because of the perfect "way" Jesus made. It also means that your spiritual performance is not a requirement for connection with your heavenly Dad. Believing in Jesus is the only way to connect with Father God.

> Without pursuing our Father as a son or daughter, we, like earthly social orphans, experience the negative effects of "separation trauma" in our daily lives.

The change in your new heavenly adoption reality is dramatic. In the New Testament period from Christ's life on earth as chronicled in the Gospels through the history and writings of the early church and apostles to the final prophetic book of Revelation, God is referenced as Father over two-hundred-fifty times. Since the historical time period covered by the Old Testament is more than four thousand years while the New Testament covers at most a century, for an equivalent reference to God as Father, the Old Testament would have to use the term more than ten thousand times rather than just nineteen. Jesus was a game-changer for everything!

That said, while through his perfect sacrifice Jesus made possible the restoration of our relationship with Father God, that relationship is voluntary. Without pursuing our Father as a son or daughter, we, like earthly social orphans, experience the negative effects of "separation trauma" in our daily lives.

Some may argue against this since through Jesus our spiritual *position* has been restored (Romans 3:23-24), transforming us from orphans to God's son or daughter, accepted in the divine family of God (John 14:18-20). But like any child, our heart's *condition* is vulnerable when lacking the sunlight of a loving touch from our heavenly Dad. If we are not cognizant of his light, our imaginations craft and embrace lies about ourselves and him.

Orphan shadows are beliefs, actions, and feelings that sons and daughters accept when they are not connected to God as their Father.

In this state, we may sing songs to God, pray, and attend church even while our hearts and minds remain guided by orphan shadows. Orphan shadows are beliefs, actions, and feelings that sons and daughters except when they are not connected to God as their Father. These shadows are where cannibalistic behaviours come from.

This is not Father God's intention for our destiny. In Christ, we carry our heavenly Father's spiritual DNA as his adopted children. Jesus had his Father's DNA through the Holy Spirit. And yet even the Son of God had to walk intimately dependant on his Dad while on this earth (John 8:28). His identity as God's Son was tested (Matthew 4:1-11). Yet he overcame and is our perfect example of what it looks like to walk as God's child on the earth (Romans 8:29). Check out the following list of how Jesus modeled what our new life as God's child should look like.

- Jesus's identity was based out of his relational connection with his Father (John 10:15, 30).

- Jesus knew he could do nothing without his Father (John 5:30).

- Jesus believed in the love his Father had for him (John 5:20).

- Jesus received authority from his Father (John 5:22, 27).

- Jesus looked for ways to honor his Father (John 8:49).

- Jesus looked for ways to show his love for his Father by obeying him (John 14:31).

- Jesus's energizing motivation and inspiration was to work to fulfill the assignments his Father gave him while on earth (John 4:34).

The four Gospels share how the Son actively chose his Dad and is our example of the only way to live a God-fulfilled life on earth. We are invited to do the same.

Our identity as God's sons and daughters is being tested every day. There is someone playing to your primal needs, masquerading as your father. He is Satan, the father of lies (John 8:44). Satan twists the truth, seducing us to meet our four primal needs on our own terms. He tickles our ears to draw us from our Father of lights (James 1:17). When our soul is not leaning into God as our Dad for help in our thoughts, feelings, and choices, by default we live in orphan shadows and quite naturally rely on social, financial, and all manner of other cannibalistic behaviors to feed our primal needs. It is a recipe for disaster.

One additional note here. In this book, I reveal the unique challenges of being physically or socially orphaned. If your origin story involves being placed, given up, apprehended, or tragically abandoned for adoption, your character, identity, and destiny are not defined by the negative characteristics of orphan shadows listed in the book. In fact, I have found that because of their own unique journeys, adoptees often bring an enlightening, deep, and intuitive understanding of being adopted into the family of God.

REFLECTIONS

- Living a Christian life without connection to God as our Father is trauma-inducing to our soul in the same way children experience the negative physical and emotional results of separation trauma.

- Jesus modeled the healthy child-Father relationship we could have with our Father. His death, burial, and resurrection opened the only way for us to have a personal connection with Father God like Jesus had when he was on earth.

- Orphan shadows are thoughts, actions or decisions arising from a son or daughter of God whose soul is not anchored in a loving, dependent relationship with God as Father.

QUESTIONS TO CONSIDER

- How central is Father God to you in your day-to-day living?

- How do you see your relationship or lack of relationship with God as your Dad affecting how you live your life?

CONNECTING WITH MY FATHER

May I invite you to join in the following prayer with me.

"Father God, thank you for sending Jesus. He is the only way back to living with you. I worship you, Lord Jesus, as my Savior and older Brother. It is because of you that I am reunited with my Dad. Please show me how to follow you in being a son/daughter of God on the earth. I recognize neither my goodness, pain, nor anything else can hinder me from walking with my heavenly Dad. I trust your work as complete. In Jesus's name, amen!"

CHAPTER SEVEN

Style Choices

$\mathcal{S}$ince the beginning of 2015, I have often been asked to teach on how God's Father heart frees us from orphan shadows. Through studying God's Word, teaching on the specifics of what this means, and growing in my own personal relationship with my heavenly Dad, I have learned that we carry a style for how we impact the world. This "style" is not a personality-based system, and it is not static or inflexible. Our impact on others flows from our connection or lack thereof with Father God.

During his ministry on Earth, Jesus shared a powerful story highlighting the importance of maintaining our relationship with God as our Father. A story commonly known as the Parable of the Prodigal Son (Luke 15:11-32). But the story actually has three characters—the prodigal son, the father, and the prodigal son's older brother. I had heard and even taught this story many times and thought I understood it fully. But within weeks of discovering God as my Dad, the parable of the Prodigal Son exploded off the pages of my Bible. I wept as Father God unwrapped it for me.

The parable begins with two sons living and working on their father's estate. But we soon learn that neither the younger nor older son know who their father really is. And while their behaviors are very different from each other, they are both polar opposites of their father's character. Let's look at the story as Jesus told it.

> A man had two sons. The younger son told his father, "I want my share of your estate now before you die." So his father agreed to divide his wealth between his sons. A few days later this younger son packed all his belongings and moved to a distant land, and there he wasted all his money in wild living. About the time his money ran out, a great famine swept over the land, and he began to starve. He persuaded a local farmer to hire him, and the man sent him into his fields to feed the pigs. The young man became so hungry that even the pods he was feeding the pigs looked good to him. But no one gave him anything. (Luke 15:11-16)

Now let's consider the younger son's request for an early inheritance. In ancient times, a son asking for the inheritance before his father's death would have been the highest form of disrespect. It would be like telling your father, "I wish you were already dead." Jesus's Jewish audience would have been horrified. A just response to such behavior would entail the father driving this disrespectful, rebellious son off the estate permanently.

But the father in this story is unlike any earthly father Jesus's audience would have ever known. Jesus describes how this father honors his son's free will, dividing up his estate and maybe even liquidating lands that had been kept in his family for generations. Undoubtedly, this would have been a painful process for the father. We can't really know, but it may even have drawn negative gossip and speculation from neighbors. But regardless of the personal cost, the father generously gave his younger son his inheritance and left him to his own decisions.

Though both sons are heirs, sharing an identity as their father's children, I call their behaviors orphan shadows because their beliefs, decisions, and attitudes don't reflect who they truly are as sons. We're going to be looking at four of these "shadows." But the first two we see here I've termed the Loner and the Dictator.

The Loner pulls away from everyone, becoming isolated and vindictive. The Dictator shows a narrow-minded form of maintaining control, striving for a self-serving agenda. Both these defaults— Loner and Dictator—are revealed in the younger son as he packs up, abandoning his caring father, to serve only his own impulses and desires, isolated and independent in a distant land.

What are the results of the younger son's choice to leave home and live his own life? In a few sentences, we read what some of us have experienced in our own lives, even after getting saved. Here are four progressive symptoms.

- A wasting of his father's inheritance.

- Famine, i.e., a shortage of sustenance.

- Dysfunctional relationships, i.e., people around him acting as takers versus givers.

- Starvation, including physical, emotional, financial, spiritual depravity.

Living in these orphan shadows leaves the son more than empty. He starts out with an inheritance he didn't earn and ends up with nothing. Not only is he starving, but his only work is feeding pigs for a living. This would have been especially humiliating for a Jew since pigs were considered ceremonially unclean animals that Jews were forbidden to eat. To the original audience listening to Jesus, this younger brother was living a disgusting life. They undoubtedly felt it was a well-deserved punishment for the son's sinful behavior and foolish choices.

But all is not lost. In the middle of his misery, the prodigal son comes to his senses. Up to this point, everything the younger son has been doing reflects a very distorted view of his father. This is true of orphan shadows operating in our own lives. However, there is a point in orphan living when a crisis brings us to our senses. Knowing he will die if he stays in that filthy, famine-struck place, the son hatches a plan, a shame plan, to return to his father.

ORPHAN PLAN

> When he finally came to his senses, he said to himself, "At home even the hired servants have food enough to spare, and here I am dying of hunger! I will go home to my father and say, 'Father, I have sinned against both heaven and you, and I am no longer worthy of being called your son. Please take me on as a hired servant.'"(Luke 15:17-19)

Recognizing he'd violated his community standards as taught by Jewish tradition, the younger son knew he couldn't just move home and expect the privileges and living standard of a son. His plan involved offering to work as a hired servant, in other words, be treated like any other employee on the estate, maybe even for the rest of his life.

How often have we found ourselves in broken places of our own making? If we're living out of orphan shadows, our broken situation can confirm the lie that in some way we are unworthy and a mistake. As orphans caught in sinful behaviour, the danger is crafting a plan to earn back our acceptance with our own efforts. Any plan we calculate on our own to bring us back closer to God will only bring more heaviness and bondage.

> If we're living out of orphan shadows, our broken situation can confirm the orphan lie that in some way we are unworthy and a mistake.

In context of your relationship with God, you may be thinking, *I need to read more, pray more, worship more to make up for my wrongs.* With some other close relationship, you may feel, *I need to serve more, forgive more, listen more, plan more to make up for my shortcomings.*

Not that there's anything wrong with these activities. But unless they come from a place of experiencing our heavenly Dad's love, they will lead us into deeper shame and bondage. This might be a time to ask ourselves what our motivation really is for "more" plans, whether in connection to God, relationships, our career, or life in general.

OUR FATHER THE RESCUER

So we now have a good grasp on what the younger son is thinking. Let's move to what is happening back on the estate. We've already seen that the father's actions to this point were culturally unconventional to Jesus's audience. And that remains true in how he reacts to his prodigal younger son coming home.

> So he [prodigal son] returned home to his father. And while he was still a long way off, his father saw him coming. Filled with love and compassion, he ran to his son, embraced him, and kissed him. His son said to him, "Father, I have sinned against both heaven and you, and I am no longer worthy of being called your son." But his father said to the servants, "Quick! Bring the finest robe in the house and put it on him. Get a ring for his finger and sandals for his feet. And kill the calf we have been fattening. We must celebrate with a feast, for this son of mine was dead and has now returned to life. He was lost, but now he is found." So the party began. (Luke 15:20-24)

For starters, his father saw him coming from "a long way off." How? Why? After all this time, was the father keeping a regular eye on the road leading to his estate, hoping that one day he'd see his younger son on that road? For a disgraced son who by all standards deserved to be completely cut off from the family, that his father would still be keeping a look-out for him is unusual enough.

Second, though the father had been dishonored by his son, when he sees him returning in the distance, the father was filled with love and compassion. He wasn't just mildly pleased to see his son.

He was overcome and overflowing with deep, gut-wrenching love for his lost son.

Finally, a prosperous landowner with servants and laborers probably didn't need to sprint down the road too often. Much less for a son who by culture and tradition (as the son's own thoughts make clear) has no right to expect anything but being treated as an outcast for his behavior, maybe even driven away without his father so much as speaking to him, or at best one more unemployed day laborer looking for a job.

Instead, the son, probably dirty and stinking from long weeks of travel, is smothered by the kisses and hugs of his overjoyed father. With his costly, reckless lifestyle and willful dishonor of his father, this son had every right to expect to spend the rest of his life in slavish repayment of his sinful behavior and wasted inheritance—if his father let him stay at all! Instead, the lavish forgiveness and celebratory love this father showed his son are remarkable in any age. Certainly to that first century Jewish audience, this entire parable would have appeared completely upside-down to the way a wronged father should treat a disobedient, wayward son.

The younger son does try to bring up his shame plan. But before he can finish describing his unworthiness, the father cuts off the son's speech of repentance. Isn't that the way it is for us? So often our repentance is tainted by shame. We curse our new identity in Jesus while saying we're sorry. We need to know our Dad's heart toward us. Christian author and speaker Graham Cooke once stated it this way:

> When the Father looks at you, he doesn't see anything wrong. He's not obsessed by sin; he's not like us. He is consumed by life!

In other words, our heavenly Father isn't rolling his eyes, withholding approval, wagging his finger, or demanding a trial period before accepting us back. Imagine this son standing on the road outside his home, the same road by which he'd left months or years earlier, scorning his father. Now, standing in the dust, wearing rancid rags, gaunt with hunger, bankrupt, friendless, and shattered, this son of Adam is encountering the true Dad, the Father of the ages, clutching him to himself.

The father's actions back his words. He calls for the finest robe to clothe his son, not just with cloth but with dignity. In ancient times, this robe would have been a special ceremonial garment, rarely worn except for special occasions like a wedding. Next the father calls for his ring, a symbol of the father's authority, used to stamp agreements in business dealings. Then he calls for sandals, because as a restored son the younger brother should not be barefoot.

Lastly, the father orders a fattened calf to be killed for a feast. The calf was a huge animal, and there weren't freezers to store meat, so this butchering was meant to be a lavish party for everyone on the estate, family, servants, laborers, maybe even the neighbors. It was time to party and celebrate! This perfect father is meeting his son's needs for belonging, provision, protection, and significance. That is your Father God's heart toward you right now.

But remember I mentioned there were three characters in this story. So far we've only met two. Let's take a look now at the older son. The one who stayed home, working hard in the fields and doing what a good son is supposed to do. But like the younger son, this older brother was also struggling with orphan shadows. The difference was that his orphan ways were more subtle and acceptable, not just to the culture of his day, but in our own as well.

Meanwhile, the older son was in the fields working. When he returned home, he heard music and dancing in the house, and he asked one of the servants what was going on. "Your brother is back," he was told, "and your father has killed the fattened calf. We are celebrating because of his safe return." The older brother was angry and wouldn't go in. His father came out and begged him, but he replied, "All these years I've slaved for you and never once refused to do a single thing you told me to. And in all that time you never gave me even one young goat for a feast with my friends. Yet when this son of yours comes back after squandering your money on prostitutes, you celebrate by killing the fattened calf!" (Luke 15:25-30)

This part of the story reveals the last two orphan shadows at which I'd like us to take a look: the Slave and the Hoarder. The Slave performs to earn acceptance without giving their heart to relationship. The Hoarder grabs, comparing and scheming, fearful of scarcity and lack. Both these orphan shadows creep into our lives when we stop allowing the Father to meet our needs as his children.

We see in this passage that the older son was disrespectful and bitter towards his father. His father's love for his younger brother threatened the older son's sense of status. He had clearly never truly known or received that love for himself personally. As a Hoarder and Slave comparing his own performance to his brother's, he recounted his good works for his father over the years. His performance was revealed for what it always had been—loveless.

Just like the younger brother, orphan shadows were devastating the older son's heart and relationships in the same areas but for different reasons. He experienced:

- Wasting his father's inheritance. In this case, the oldest son never really enjoyed his inheritance because he was too caught up in his own efforts of performance.

- Famine. That he was experiencing a shortage of love, joy, and freedom was revealed in his response when grace was extended to his brother.

- Dysfunctional relationships. Caught in a relationship based on striving to achieve his father's approval through good works, the older brother could not embrace his father as a son.

- Starvation. The older brother lived in emotional and spiritual emptiness, refusing to rejoice over his brother's restoration, because he did not interpret reality through his Father's relationship lens.

When we relate to our Father based on our own performance, we are unable to enjoy all he has given us.

When we relate to our Father based on our own performance, we are unable to enjoy all he has given us. Just like the oldest brother, we will secretly resent those who receive Father God's grace. But thankfully, that isn't the end of the story nor the final message Jesus was communicating to that first-century audience or to us today.

REFLECTIONS

- Both sons in Jesus's parable hurt themselves and others because they didn't know and accept their father's heart, resulting in Loner, Dictator, Slave, and Hoarder reactions and behaviors.

- The father in Jesus's parable reflects how perfectly our Father relates to all his children.

QUESTIONS TO CONSIDER

- What aspects of yourself do you see in the two sons' reactions and/or behaviors?

- How have you been personally impacted by your Father God's loving responses to your orphan shadows?

CONNECTING WITH MY FATHER

May I invite you to join in the following prayer with me.

"Father God, how amazing and loving you are to everyone! Your tender care and proactive compassion are what I need. Please help me to forgive myself where I have acted out in orphan ways in my life. I invite you to push aside any shadows I am holding on to. As you do this in me, please help me to accept that in Christ I have your nature and am able to reflect who you are. Thank you, Father, for delivering me from orphan shadows. I am who you say I am— your child. In Jesus's name, amen."

CHAPTER EIGHT

Impact Drivers

*L*et's take a look at the final outcome of these two "orphan" brothers both seeking a restored relationship with their father.

> His father said to him, "Look, dear son, you have always stayed by me, and everything I have is yours. We had to celebrate this happy day. For your brother was dead and has come back to life! He was lost, but now he is found!" (Luke 15:31-32)

Just as the parable reveals the father's deep love and forgiveness for his younger prodigal son, so Jesus ends his parable with the father communicating his deep, abiding love for his eldest son. He reaffirms the older son's valued status as the heir of his remaining estate (that his father might now decide to give part of the older son's inheritance to his prodigal brother might have been one worry of the older son in seeing his brother so warmly welcomed back!) He then implores his son to forgive his brother.

How beautiful the response of this father to both of his sons' orphan shadow ways. Our heavenly Dad is all about relationship. He is pursuing our hearts and has been since Adam and Eve left the family estate, covered in sin and shame. Let's take one more look at this parable in the context of how it highlights the way our Father God relates to us.

Helper: In the beginning of the story when the younger son asks for his inheritance, instead of punishing him, the father willingly liquidates assets and gives him the younger son's portion (Luke 15:12). The Bible refers to God as our Helper (Psalm 54:4; John 14:26; Hebrews 13:6).

Advocate: When the younger son returns, rather than punishing or demanding repayment from his son, the father runs out to forgive him and celebrates his son's return to his position of honor (Luke 15:20, 22-24). The Bible refers to our God as our Advocate (John 14:16; 1 John 2:1).

Giver: Beyond merely forgiving his son, the father restores him by giving him the status symbols of authority and sonship (Luke 15:22-24). The Bible refers to God as our Giver (John 3:16; James 1:17; 2 Corinthians 8:9).

Reconciler: Not content with just forgiving the younger son himself, the father steps out to encourage others to reconcile with the younger son (Luke 15:31-32). The Bible refers to God as our Reconciler (Romans 5:10; Colossians 1:19-20; 2 Corinthians 5:18).

I will never forget when Father God pointed out to me that there were not three sons in this parable but two. I realized I'd mentally created three categories of people—the rebellious younger son, the hypocritical older son, and people like me who were neither of the two sons. How blind I was! As I've grown fond of my Father God's presence, I have discovered the different orphan shadows of both sons operating through me. It doesn't matter. Whether it is the Dictator, Loner, Slave, or Hoarder, they are no match for his love.

IMPACT STYLES

Our heavenly Dad has been pursuing broken humanity in our spiritual orphanhood for thousands of years, as documented in the Old Testament. All the biblical characters during this time period didn't have Jesus as mediator between themselves and the Father (1 Timothy 2:5), so they lived as spiritual orphans. Didn't Jesus say, "no one can come to the Father except through me" (John 14:6)?

> It wasn't possible before Jesus to know God fully as Father because it took a perfect Son to introduce a perfect Father.

Consider God's great concern for the treatment of literal earthly orphans and widows in the Old Testament. Though humanity had shut him out, he still created laws and reminded Israel to treat them well (Exodus 22:22; Isaiah 1:17). Why? Because his *being* is God, but part of his identity is a Father carrying a Father's loving heart. It wasn't possible before Jesus to know God fully as Father because it took a perfect Son to introduce a perfect Father. Jesus came and was the way, truth, and life of the Father (John 14:6) to restore the human race back to God's family (John 3:16).

That said, this period of history was not a waste of time. God in his divine irony unfolds Old Testament history to help us recognize our own orphan ways so that we can choose to grow up into full adoption. I love how Father God penned the Old

Testament, revealing people's flaws, victories, and shortcomings. These historical accounts reveal God opening the door for his only Son Jesus to make a way to our heavenly Dad through himself.

They also provide us with rich, detailed biographies of spiritual orphans to guide and remind us. We see a stark contrast between past orphan living and our new real identity in Christ as God's sons and daughters. In the following chapters we will learn more about orphan shadows from the life stories of Jonah, Samson, Jephthah, and Jacob.

After my eyes were opened to see and know God as my Dad, I began seeing orphan shadows throughout Old Testament stories. As mentioned earlier, these orphan identities are the Dictator, Loner, Slave, and Hoarder. Each of these four orphan shadows display a variety of subtle cannibalistic behaviours. If we accept them long enough, rely on and perfect using them to satisfy our primal needs, we become unable to distinguish our broken personality and habits from our new identity in Christ.

But the amazing thing about what Jesus did for us is that he gave us a new nature that reflects who our Father really is (Ephesians 4:24). Because of his death and resurrection, we inherit our Father's opposite responses to orphan shadow tendencies: helping, advocating, giving, and reconciling.

I call these God-approaches to sin and conflict Impact Drivers. To make an impact is to have a strong effect on someone or something. Jesus was impactful. Whether people agreed with him or not, they felt the impact of his actions and words.

A driver is defined as a factor that causes something to happen. As mentioned earlier, Jesus's relationship with his Father was his only motivator for the impactful things he did. These Impact

Drivers are a radically different approach to our world's problems. They are powerful traits of God eternally established in Father God's children through Jesus Christ, not earned through our good performance.

In the following chapters, we'll be reviewing characteristics of the four orphan shadows: Dictator, Loner, Slave, and Hoarder. I will share my own epiphanies from witnessing orphan shadows at work in my life.

We will also examine characteristics of the four Impact Drivers: Helper, Advocate, Giver, and Reconciler. I will share how my relationship with Father God transformed me, causing the orphan shadows to fade while activating new motivations inside of me for greater impact in my relationships and work responsibilities. This gradual change starts by believing that Jesus's finished sacrifice on the cross is enough for me. In Christ, I am a Helper, Advocate, Giver, and Reconciler regardless of the shadows I cast around me.

> In Christ, I am a Helper, Advocate, Giver, and Reconciler regardless of the shadows I cast around me.

The Bible declares that we are new creations in Christ (2 Corinthians 5:17). As God's children, we partake of his nature (2 Peter 1:4). So for our Dictator reactions, we've been given a helping heart. For our Loner attitudes, we have in Christ a reconciling ability. For a Slave mindset, we move toward being an advocate for the helpless. And for our Hoarder habits, Jesus gives us the heart of a giver.

If I say that I believe I'm a new creation in Christ, yet in a pinch or crisis my actions and attitudes reflect one of the orphan identities, it is because I have nurtured my primal needs without my heavenly Father's help. We need to stop adopting other identities and start accepting and living our lives as God's adopted ones. In doing so, we learn the freedom we have in Jesus (Galatians 5:1).

I have discovered all of these orphan shadows in my own life, but amazingly, I find they effortlessly dissolve as I learn how to do living with God as my Dad. All my needs of belonging, provision, protection, and significance are perfectly touched by him. My heart softens, and I am free to live with a peace that is beyond human explanation (Philippians 4:7).

As we will soon see, the degree to which you grow up into your adoption, choosing connection with your Father, is the degree to which orphan shadows lose sway on you, replaced by the powerful Impact Drivers of God's Spirit. This is the key to rising above social cannibalism. As you begin to see things in a new way, remember that the only antidote to orphan shadows is your Dad's heart for you. It's that simple.

Satan's power was stripped away through Jesus's death, burial, and resurrection. Our adversary doesn't have to work too hard creating chaos in a world filled with billions of overwhelmed, disconnected spiritual orphans. Perhaps we've given Satan too much credit. It can be easy to attribute wars, conflicts, and painful, broken experiences to dark spiritual forces when many actions and their negative consequences are driven by the human insecurity and anxiety of living without our heavenly Dad.

Only our Father can transmit true dignity and worth in real time. No other substitute comes even close to sufficient. Without him, we slip into shame and receive the broadcast: *I am unworthy! I am a mistake! I am lacking!* These unconscious conclusions drive us to strive under orphan shadows that best suit us or our situation.

In contrast, Father God does away with shame by answering the deep primal needs of our being. As God's children, our best days are ahead. When we learn to live with Father God as Jesus modeled for us, we will provide the dignity, stability, and hope our world desperately needs.

As you learn about these four orphan types, know one thing. They are not you! If you recognize a behavior operating in your life, remember these are only shadows. On a sunny day in an open parking lot, would my wife kiss my cheek or kneel on the asphalt to kiss the shadow my body leaves on the pavement?

Of course, she would plant her lips on my cheek because the shadow on the pavement is not the real me. Likewise, the real you is who you are in Christ—God's girl or boy! As we grow up in our relationship with our heavenly Dad, he gently communicates to us who we really are. Are you ready to be the real you?

REFLECTIONS

- The father in Jesus's parable reflects how our Father relates to us. He redeems brokenness with a loving response shown in the ways he lavishly gave, advocated, reconciled, and helped his sons despite how he was treated.

- As children of God, in Christ we inherit our Father's nature for lavishly loving ourselves and others.

QUESTIONS TO CONSIDER

- Where have you seen God's grace help you respond as the father did in Jesus's parable?

- In what areas or relationships of your life do you struggle believing that Father God has replaced your shadows for his Impact Drivers?

CONNECTING WITH MY FATHER

May I invite you to join in the following prayer with me.

"Father God, how amazing and loving you are to everyone! Your tender care and proactive compassion are what I need. Please show me how you have been a Giver, Reconciler, Advocate, and Helper to me in my life. As you show me, please help me to accept that in Christ I have your nature and am able to reflect who you are. I believe, Father God, that you have Impact Driver adventures laid out my future. Thank you that I am not alone but you are with me. In Jesus's name, amen!"

CHAPTER NINE

The Dictator

*W*e've already discussed that each "orphan shadow" is an identity mindset, a way of thinking. We stay under these spiritual orphan shadows in an attempt to meet our core design needs as children. Consider an earthly orphaned child with no parents or protectors creating a safe environment for them. To survive, they learn to depend on themselves alone.

Even if we are blessed with amazing parents or family, they can never give us the level of security we were designed to need as a spiritual being. We may have accepted Jesus as our Savior. But if we are still living outside of an ongoing reliance on our heavenly Father, allowing him to parent us, allowing his perfect love and security to fill every crack in our hearts, we *will* automatically rely on and live out of reactive strategies, attempting to manipulate situations and people around us to create our own safety and security.

The first such shadow cast over spiritual orphans is what I call the Dictator. Sadly, we too often forget that when Father God created us, he gave us dominion over everything on earth except one another (Genesis 1:26-28). In consequence, domination, subjugation, and using power for control have been common in all cultures on every continent, whether ancient tribal chieftains in Africa, medieval European kings, or modern fascists like Stalin and Hitler.

Even at emotional and social levels, our families, business practices, educational institutions, and governments exert some form of power and control. Leadership is necessary, and order is good. But what is so often missing in our world is selfless love.

Surely I'm not a dictator! many of us may be thinking. In fact, we may pride ourselves in our agreeableness and civility. But we are not referencing personality or even action here. I've witnessed respected, devout women who sit quietly in a back pew at church, yet exert subtle, continuous control over church leadership, family, and/ or husband. Such a woman may not even realize those under her influence are caught in an emotional lock-down year after year. As with earthly orphans, the Dictator mindset has been unconsciously integrated into her identity. A common justification one hears is: "I can't help it. This is just who I am. I mean the best for everyone."

Every child longs to feel significant. Those with unconscious Dictator mindsets strive for significance by using their own efforts, influence, and gifts to accomplish great things. Life can only work for them on their terms because they have crafted a world requiring themselves to always be in control. In contrast, Jesus set a perfect example in surrendering control to the only One who could meet that need. When confronted with death, he prayed to his Father, "Not my will but yours be done" (Luke 22:42). A Dictator mindset cannot pray this prayer and mean it.

A Dictator identity also strives to control its environment, situation, or relationships. Just as an orphan child searches for belonging, so the Dictator mentality has an unconscious, insatiable craving to be needed by others and/or God. Dictators will use money, advice, service, leadership ability, natural or spiritual gifting, or insight to make themselves indispensable to individuals or groups.

All good things, of course. But when they are not grounded in Father God's heart, even well-intentioned efforts turn into control, conflict, or self-driven adulation. Indicators of a Dictator orphan mindset include the following.

- **Striving:** Laboring to find security and satisfaction through something/someone else instead of leaning into Father God.

- **Control:** Trying to be more, take more, or require others to be more than the Father is requiring of them in any situation.

- **Judgmental, resentful, and unforgiving:** Refusing to view or relate with others the way Father God does.

- **Savior complex:** Acting and/or speaking in ways that exalt ourselves as the answer.

- **Perfectionist:** Making demands of self and others Father God is not making.

- **Selfishness:** Putting our own needs, gifts, and interests before everyone else's.

- **Narrow mindedness:** An inability to genuinely explore viewpoints beyond our own.

- **Self-pity:** Anger and self-centered sadness that our view of life, people, or things does not agree with our Father's.

The above characteristics are broad and relate to us all in different ways. We may carry a mindset of superiority, driving us to mistrust another's ability, leading us to compulsive competitiveness and/or striving in situations. This can leave us seeing everything through a win/lose lens. We find ourselves fighting to fix people who don't care what we think and don't want to be fixed. It hurts to lose in a conversation, discussion, or interaction because our personal worth is unconsciously tied to our opinion of being right.

For some of us, it also means feeling the need to control situations or people. The assumption of the Dictator mindset is: "I see things better than others." So we overtly or covertly micromanage others. We feel we must act now to ensure survival, so we may step in prematurely, asserting our gifts for the good of others. We then misinterpret people's reactions to our gifts, advice, and efforts (or they misinterpret our intentions!), resulting in hurt, judgment, and unforgiveness. Ultimately, this mindset aggravates relationships, pushing away the very people we need most.

GETTING OUT OF THE BOAT

Let's take a trip down imagination lane. Once upon a time, you lived in a country that was fragmented and leaderless, stuck in mismanagement and declining wealth. Your greatest enemy nation to the north has subtly turned to subjugate your country in ever-increasing ways. No one is safe. Your countrymen are filled with tension. Whether shopping, going to work, or attending public meetings, people are anxious, disturbed, and frustrated. The problem is that no one can see a way forward. Even church leaders and businessmen hang their heads in humiliation, fear, and silence.

In the middle of all this, you have a spiritual encounter with God giving you a picture of what he wants to do. You begin publicly predicting a coming epic redemption with radical reversal of fortunes and prosperity for your nation. You write a book, travel, and teach. You work hard to spread the news. Though many hear your message, few believe it is possible. Many even laugh at the futility of such grandiose dreams.

Then, denying the impossible odds, a series of events changes the course of your nation—politically, socially, and economically. As national enemies wither in disarray, your country takes back land stolen many years earlier. Local economies flourish while government is stabilized at every level. People begin talking optimistically about their children's future. Your countrymen are filled with pride, vibrancy, and self-respect.

In the middle of this, everyone witnesses the miraculous fulfillment of your predictions. You are now held in great esteem with people turning to you for advice, prayers, and predictions. You are soon a nationally-successful high-profile minister, enjoying prestige, security, and wealth. You are living the good life. What could possibly go wrong?

JONAH

Does this narrative sound familiar? This is the biblical story of the prophet Jonah, who successfully predicted the restoration of the Northern Kingdom of Israel (2 King 14:25-27). The golden age that followed included increased political and social stability as Israel's historic enemy Assyria faltered with internal problems. During this period, lost territory was reclaimed and wealth returned to the Jewish people.

With everything going so well, how did things get so messy for Jonah? Remember our discussion of identity a few chapters back. Identity is how we view ourselves, which in turn determines how we respond to God, ourselves, and others. We can be rich or poor, but if we don't have a correct view of ourselves, we will always be searching. We can be devout or uncommitted, but if we don't know ourselves, there will always be a deep sense of restlessness. We can be gifted or ordinary, but if we don't see ourselves as Father God sees us, we will always wonder what our purpose is.

In the story of Jonah, we witness Father God pursuing the heart of his orphan child. When life is good, our orphan default identities are often veiled. But when crisis or distress arises, our true view of ourselves quickly becomes evident. That was the case in Jonah's situation. Everything was great in his life and ministry until God asked Jonah to do the unthinkable. Jonah was to go to Nineveh and preach that because of their wickedness God would overthrow their city in forty days (Jonah 1:1-2; 3:1-4).

Now you'd think Jonah would be happy to deliver a message that Israel's greatest national threat was about to be destroyed. After all, the Assyrian powerhouse had defeated and subjugated surrounding nations through visceral fear. They skinned their enemy's bodies alive. They impaled defeated foes on poles and piled heaps of their heads outside city gates to remind defeated survivors what would happen if they decided to fight for freedom. In fact, the very name Nineveh means *city of blood*.

So why wouldn't Jonah jump at the chance to rub it in to his country's greatest enemy that God was about to wipe them out? Jonah himself gives us the answer after God intervenes, Jonah finally obeys, and in response to his powerful preaching, the city of Nineveh repents of its wickedness. In fact, in context it is clear Jonah raised this objection when God first gave the prophet his marching orders.

> He [Jonah] prayed to the Lord, "Isn't this what I said,
> Lord, when I was still at home? . . . I knew that you
> are a gracious and compassionate God, slow to an-
> ger and abounding in love, a God who relents from
> sending calamity. (Jonah 4:2-3, NIV)

In other words, Jonah knew there was only one reason God would send him to Nineveh to preach their impending destruction. God, in his mercy, was giving the Assyrians one last chance to repent. Otherwise, he could have just wiped Nineveh out without warning. Jonah's reaction makes clear how shocking he found this mission. "Say what, God? You want me to give an opportunity for repentance and mercy to a city dripping with the innocent blood of surrounding countries, including your chosen people?"

Jonah's next steps in response to God's voice were more than a slight overreaction. Instead of heading to Nineveh, about seven hundred miles north, he bought a very expensive one-way boat ticket to Tarshish, a remote port on the Iberian Peninsula over twenty-four-hundred miles to the west. In other words, more than three times the distance of where he'd been sent and in the complete opposite direction.

Why was his response so extreme? I've heard it speculated that Jonah didn't really know God. But Jonah must have known God since God spoke through him as his prophet and chose him for the mission to Nineveh. The problem was that Jonah worshipped, followed, and knew God to a degree, but he didn't truly understand who God is. Because of this, Jonah operated with the mindset of a Dictator, attempting to control his future and the future of the Assyrians.

I'd like to stop for a moment here to emphasize a vital principle that applies to all of us, including Jonah. You can't know who you are until you know who your Father is, and you don't know your Father until you experience his heart. As you get to know your Father, he speaks empowering definition and heavenly identity into you, releasing deep security into your being. As his son or daughter, you just don't need to be a Dictator anymore.

DEATH WISH #1

As the story unfolds, Jonah continues to reveal the mindset of a spiritual orphan. Living out of a spiritual orphan identity means justifying distorted living and half-truths. And so Jonah bolts (Jonah 1:3). He was on a ship headed to Tarshish in the middle of the Mediterranean Sea when God sent a violent storm to confront his heart. As a Dictator, Jonah was unable to surrender his plans to God. So we shouldn't be surprised that his first death wish was centered around control (Jonah 1:4-15).

> You can't know who you are until you know who your Father is, and you don't know your Father until you experience his heart.

Discovering that Jonah was the cause of the storm, the sailors asked him what they should do. Jonah's response was to have them throw him into the sea so the sea would calm. Now obviously, asking to be thrown overboard in the middle of a raging Mediterranean Sea tempest was tantamount to a death wish. Dog-paddling wouldn't cut it. Jonah could instead have repented and promised God to turn around at the next port. But he preferred to die and maintain control than submit to God's plans for his life.

This is the nature of a spiritual orphan. When confronted, it becomes irrational. It says, "I care more about what I think and what I'm doing than what God is thinking and doing."

This aspect of the Dictator mentality grows quietly and slowly until it is a regular way of living. The wrong views we carry about ourselves and God become defaults in our decision-making. We honor God with our lips, but our hearts are far from him (Matthew 15:8). He is our Father God, so we should always see ourselves as sons and daughters first. This empowers us to surrender to God in uncertain situations.

DEATH WISH #2

As the story continues to unfold, God responds in love and mercy. Even his first death wish is beyond Jonah's control. The sailors do throw him overboard, but God sends a huge fish to swallow him, saving Jonah's life and eventually leading him to change course back to his original mission (Jonah 1:15-3:1). When he finally arrives in Nineveh and preaches God's warning of impending judgment, the entire population radically repents. God in turn shows mercy, relenting from destroying Nineveh (Jonah 3:10). Great, right?

Wrong! At least in Jonah's estimation. He is furious that God would forgive Israel's enemies without his permission. Once again, his mentality is one of control. In this case, that control involves wanting God to carry out *his* desire to destroy his nation's enemy.

In fact, he is so furious that he voices a second death wish, reminding God that God's propensity for love, mercy, and compassion was why he hadn't wanted to come in the first place. So God might as well just kill him now as he'd rather be dead than not have his predictions of judgment and destruction on Nineveh come to pass (Jonah 4:1-3).

Do you see the torment of slipping into Dictator identity? Living with this mindset is a hard way to live. There is no rest because we must always strive to control people and outcomes, judging others, living resentfully when things turn out differently than we hoped. We can operate this way without anyone knowing it for a while, but eventually resentment and anger leak out.

Having a wrong identity means we are led to focus on the wrong things. As Dictators, we get caught focusing on what God is not doing at the expense of seeing what he *is* doing. This leads us to host our very own self-pity party, leading to more frustration. If only Jonah had known Father God's heart, he would have known who he was called to be.

DEATH WISH #3

Caught in a Dictator mindset, Jonah refused to accept God's decision to spare Nineveh. Instead, he set up an observatory camp outside the city, still hoping for Nineveh's eventual destruction (Jonah 4:5). Even in Jonah's grumpy, judgmental state, Father God loved him so much that he caused a leafy plant to grow to give Jonah shelter from the heat. This improved Jonah's attitude until God sent a worm to eat the plant, leaving Jonah to the mercy of a blazing sun and hot, arid wind (Jonah 4:6-8).

Once again, Jonah angrily expresses a death wish, telling God, "Death is certainly better than living like this!" (Jonah 4:9)

When we walk in selfishness, we care more about what Father God gives us than who he is. We care more about our thoughts, well-being, ideas, opinions, and plans than others. Though Jonah had already experienced God's mercy and care when God rescued him from drowning, he was miserable because he didn't share his Father's loving, compassionate heart. Instead, he drifted further into fatherless living and an ungrateful, striving Dictator mindset.

Jonah isn't the only person with Dictator orphan tendencies we see in Scripture. Another Old Testament personage caught in Dictator living was King Saul, Israel's first anointed king (1 Samuel 10:1, 21-24). In several situations, Saul's need for efficiency, self-reliance, and control drove him to do things his own way rather than obey God (I Samuel 13; 15:26-28). In consequence, God took away Saul's anointed status.

In studying Saul's case, it is interesting to note the king's sincerity and apparent good intentions in impatiently taking control (1 Samuel 13:8-13; 15:13-19). I have to ask myself how many times I've disobeyed God out of the sincerity of my own good intentions. In all its expressions, the Dictator mindset strives for control, ensnaring Dictator orphans in a narrow-minded view that they are right and must act on their own rather than waiting for God's direction.

REFLECTIONS

- Though often filled with good intentions, Dictator orphan shadow mindsets revolve around needing to build control in order to feel secure.

- Not experiencing Father God's heart drove Jonah to try to control how he died, who he helped, and who God helped.

- Having an orphan identity misleads us to raise up our own agenda and to focus on what God is not doing or not giving us in our lives.

QUESTIONS TO CONSIDER

- In what areas of my life do I struggle to release control to God?

- What do I believe about myself and God in these areas?

- How much do I make others around me feel comfortable to share, take the lead, or disagree with me?

CONNECTING WITH MY FATHER

May I invite you to join me in praying the following prayer.

"Father God, you are Lord of all things. I worship you as my own personal Dad. I acknowledge that the safest place for me to be is when I allow you to be in control. Please forgive me for enjoying my agendas more than you. I want to know you more so that the focus of my heart and mind is guided by your love. I invite you to show yourself to me. In Jesus's name, amen!"

CHAPTER TEN

The Helper

When Father God is our supreme reference point for everything in our lives, the need to control or dictate is completely lost because we know that his loving intention for our lives is far better than anything we could accomplish by ourselves. You may be thinking, "Hey, you don't know me, David. I'm the biggest Dictator on the planet!"

Maybe! I can certainly identify with that. Thankfully, if we are in Christ, then we have his nature that allows us to reflect to the world who God really is. I mentioned before that each wrong "orphan shadow" mindset has its opposite mindset and behavior. I've termed these Impact Drivers, each reflected in who Jesus was and how he lived on this earth. As these Impact Drivers replace the original orphan mindsets in our lives, that transformation allows us to increasingly reflect to the world who God really is.

The Impact Driver corresponding to Dictator is that of Helper. What exactly does that look like? Here are some of the signature characteristics of a Helper.

- **Server**: Being with our heavenly Dad leads us to begin wanting to do what he does, serving and blessing others without reservation.

- **Gap Filler**: Responding to needs, inefficiencies, or weakness delights us because it allows us opportunity to reflect what our Father is like.

- **Listener:** Recognizing that Father God has the answer, our part in every crisis is to first listen and to honor others the way our Father does.

- **Encourager:** Acting and/or speaking in ways that empower others toward breakthrough/success.

- **Practical:** As our Father directs us, putting others' needs, gifts, and interests before our own in big and small ways.

- **Open hearted:** Being with our heavenly Dad causes us to genuinely explore viewpoints beyond our own, to release wrongs committed against us, and to trust our/others' future to God.

- **Contented Optimism:** Joy, hope, and peace arising from viewing our life and relationships the way our Father views them.

When I became aware of the four different orphan shadows, I found it hard to identify the Dictator shadow in my own life. This was in part because I'd been a timid boy growing up and was typically the kid who didn't get into trouble, the teacher's pet, the peacemaker at work, on the playground, or with friends. I didn't want to control anyone. In fact, my dad had always taught me to stand up for the little guy against bullies.

That all changed one day when I fought a bully—only to become the bully. Though shy, I was also one of the strongest, fastest boys in my grade. In late fall 1981, I'd advanced to grade four, the highest grade in my school wing, which in turn meant I was now one of the strongest, fastest kids around. This left me feeling a cautious self-assurance.

One day after school, I was walking home when I noticed Michael, a mischievous third-grade boy, laughing and pushing two much smaller second-graders. They were cowering away from Michael, uncomfortable and afraid. Anger burned in me. I felt justified to act. Running toward the group, I yelled, "Stop pushing them, Michael! Leave them alone!"

With an amused smirk, Michael stepped back. I didn't. Pushing Michael hard, I demanded, "What's your problem? Why don't you pick on someone your own size?"

The smirk faded, and Michael muttered, "All right, I'll leave them alone. Sorry!"

But that wasn't enough for me. I grabbed at Michael. *I'll show you what it feels like!* Though he was bigger than his victims, he was smaller and lighter than me, and as I shoved him hard, I saw fear flicker in his eyes. The last push drove him to the ground, his body rolling into the ditch behind us.

"I'm sorry, David!" he cried out. "I'm sorry. Please stop!"

I'm sad to say I didn't stop. Following him into the ditch, I held his jacket collar with one hand while my other hand flashed punches at his head. Kneeling on the ground, Michael grabbed at my hand, trying to ward me off as he screamed, "Stop! Help! Stop!"

By now, a group of other kids had gathered to watch. I finally stopped and walked away triumphantly, leaving Michael's shamed ego and bruised face behind me. What had driven me to such ugly behaviour? Sure, it's good to stand up to a bully. But to become one? How could this happen?

Every human being can revert to ugly, dominating behavior when they are overwhelmed by their visceral insecurity.

Every human being can revert to ugly, dominating behavior when they are overwhelmed by their visceral insecurity. As mentioned earlier, a child is pre-made with a primal hunger for a loving parent to show them value, protection, and provision for their needs. When these core needs aren't met, we turn to "survival" reactions, which include controlling, dominating, even bullying.

After awhile, these default behaviors become so natural to us that we assume they are a part of our personality. In turn, others around us often build their own orphan strategies to cope with our reactions. Unfortunately, this lifestyle is unsatisfying and restless and often keeps us locked in suspicion and misunderstanding.

I remember walking home from the bullying crime scene feeling a superiority mixed with something uncomfortably foreign and ugly throbbing in my stomach. I tried to ignore it, but it quietly spread like vehicle fumes creeping in through an open window. I hated that feeling. I hated what I had done. Shame crept over me like a cloud until my fourth-grade heart vowed with all the determination I could muster to control and hide my anger from then on.

And so began my journey of being "Mr. Nice Guy." I tried not to be aggressive, confrontational, overpowering, or dominating in any way. Those who knew me saw me as a peacekeeper. But though I looked clean and shiny on the outside, I eventually learned that my Dictator compulsions expressed themselves in more subtle, passive-aggressive, and socially acceptable ways.

PRESUMPTION AND PERCEPTIONS

In relationships, my Dictator tendencies reflected in asserting control through quiet guilting, playing the humble victim, and being passive-aggressive. Withdrawing from my wife when offended was a Dictator's way of controlling my deep feelings of insecurity. If we're honest, we've all had Dictator moments. Being aloof with a spouse or friend because we feel unjustly treated. Pretending to listen to a co-worker's ideas just to gain their support. Being irritated and judgmental with someone for not following our unsolicited advice to fix their problems. These are all Dictator behaviors.

But for me it didn't stop there. How I managed my time was another subtle opportunity to display a Dictator mindset. Jesus was my God, but in my internal world I built clear pathways for where and how God could direct my life. Anything deviating from my neatly fitting presumptions and parameters just simply couldn't be from God. I constructed an internal timeline of goals for my life. When I would be married. How much I would earn and by when. How big my house would be and how often I would go on vacation. How big my ministry would be. You get the picture.

Not that there's anything wrong with goal-setting. To this day, I teach clients in my consulting practice how to set goals. But goal-setting in the hands of someone who doesn't know their Father brings little permanent satisfaction, always requiring more service, a bigger challenge. And so the cycle continues. Dictating our life's direction on our own is a futile endeavor of idolatry, leading us away from our heavenly Dad.

Money was another open door for the Dictator mindset to demand control in my own life. Growing up as a pastor's kid, I'd seen our family live through sparse times, so I was keen to rectify this. In my twenties, my solution was to try to become a millionaire, thinking I could then use those earnings to fund my ministry activities. I began working toward becoming a certified insurance agent. My spreadsheet of financial goals included a weekly target of closed deals that over eight years would leave me more than a million dollars. I would then have financial freedom and personal security. Perfect, right?

Then one night as I was packing up paperwork and admiring my resourcefulness, I heard God's loving nudge. "Looks great, David. But I have one question. The day after you've reached your goal of building this million-dollar portfolio, would you be willing to give it away if I asked you?"

"Yes, absolutely!" was my automatic response. Then I realized this would defeat my plan of building a big enough estate so I'd be free to do ministry on my terms. It was no use debating. I understood good and well what God was asking. Some of us may be called by our Father to build an estate for his kingdom. But I knew in that moment my activities were not motivated by my Father's love or call. A few weeks later I resigned from my position.

It's not that our Father doesn't want us to prosper. Quite the opposite. But my Dictator tendencies were aimed at controlling my future to ensure my needs would be met. You'd think I'd have learned my lesson. But until I allowed Father God to meet my deepest needs through real relationship, my "orphan shadow" defaults for decisions, relationships, and opportunities led me toward cozy, socially-palatable control.

This same Dictator scenario played itself out in dozens of failed business attempts, a couple ministry initiatives, and different friendships. I assumed that because God is loving and won't control us against our will, I could pursue anything I wanted. Of course I prayed, inviting God into my plans. But they were still my plans, motivated by logical self-interest rather than Father God's love.

These plans didn't require me to sit on my heavenly Dad's lap and listen to his heart. These plans always put me in the center, generally leaving me feeling superior but battling depression and insecurity. If only I'd asked my Father, "How do you feel about this? What do you want to show me?"

But to do that, I needed to give up control. Because allowing God to be our Father means giving up control.

SHIFTING FROM DICTATOR TO HELPER

Since my encounter with Father God in California, I'd stumbled on a therapeutic tool called PACE. This tool was developed by clinical psychologist Dr. Dan Hughes to guide foster parents in helping children traumatized by abuse and neglect. The acronym stands for:

- **Playfulness:** Enjoying the child, creating lightness, being spontaneous with no unspoken agenda.

- **Acceptance:** Showing the child they have value beyond their wrong behaviour by recognizing and exploring difficult feelings and emotions.

- **Curiosity:** Helping the child understand their internal motivations by authentically seeking out the child's experiences.

- **Empathy:** Expressing compassion and an unspoken message to the child that it is a privilege to stand with them through hard times.

When applied in family environments, PACE is used to focus on the whole child, not simply negative behaviours. This tool has helped children move to greater wholeness by helping them feel more secure, enabling greater self-discovery, and empowering them to make better decisions. To my amazement, this tool also reflected how Father God had been relating to my own insecurities and fears around issues of provision, protection, belonging, and significance.

The Gospels demonstrate how these same four characteristics were reflected in the life of Jesus, which in turn mean they reflect our Father's character since Jesus is the perfect representation of what the Father is like (Hebrews 1:3; Colossians 1:15; John 14:7-9). The following are just a few examples in the life of Jesus while he lived on the earth.

Playfulness: Full of joy, Jesus laughed with his disciples (Luke 10:21). His attitude and demeaner made it easy for children wanting to come to him (Matthew 19:13). His opponents accused him of being a glutton and drunk because he could enjoy feasting and merrymaking with "sinners" (Matthew 11:19; Luke 5:30-31).

Acceptance: Jesus showed unconditional acceptance to marginalized people. He praised the widow who gave her last pennies to God (Mark 12:41), showed mercy to the woman caught in adultery (John 8:1-11), forgave and defended a woman labelled a "sinner" who anointed his feet with expensive oil in public (Luke 7:36-50).

Curiosity: Over one hundred-thirty-five times in the four Gospels, Jesus asked questions and many times answered a question with a question. On occasions like the Samaritan woman at the well (John

4:4-26), Jesus built relationships by showing interest in people's personal lives. He didn't presume things about those close to him but pursued their understanding, inviting them to share their perspectives (John 1:38; Mark 8:27-29).

Empathy: Jesus was constantly moved by compassion for people (Matthew 14:14). He taught people because of the compassion he felt for them (Mark 6:34). He healed people out of compassion (Matthew 20:20-34).

I am so grateful our Father doesn't try to fix us or pursue a co-dependant relationship with us just to fill his own need for significance or belonging. He is bigger than our weaknesses and isn't fazed by our immaturities. Being with our heavenly Dad melts our hearts, transforming and pushing back Dictator shadows with his light. Hanging out with Father God also shifts us from Dictator tendencies to helping tendencies. We no longer need to control. Instead, we can honor the weak, different, and even the offensive around us and bless their journey even when it hurts us.

More than that, we learn to let Father God lead us, trusting his heart, wisdom, and lordship. This doesn't happen all at once. It is a relational process of our heavenly Dad keeping pace with our maturing process just as a loving, patient father keeps pace beside his toddler as the toddler is learning to walk rather than pushing his child to learn, grow, and go faster than little legs can handle.

For me, this was a new experience and profound revelation as it came in total opposition to the religious performance I'd been living. The Bible tells us that in the incarnation, God humbled himself to take on the form and limitations of a man (John 1:14; Philippians 2:5-8). Have you ever stopped to think what it must have been like for the omnipotent God of the universe, who can be and do and move at any speed he wishes, to slow himself down to the limited pace of a fragile, mortal human being?

Similarly, when Father God entered into my life journey, he patiently slowed himself to keep pace beside me, not driving me to mature more quickly or condemning my sluggishness at being transformed. He was relational and curious, drawing me out even when my own tendency was to drive myself to "do better." His compassion and empathy with my humanity was freeing.

My weakness and slowness was not a problem for him. This set me free, not to resent my own weakness, but to find my Father right alongside me in the journey, keeping pace with me at my speed.

PARTNERING AS GOD'S HELPER

As we relate more and more to our Father God, we slowly shift to reflect his DNA in our lives. And since his DNA includes being a Helper (1 John 2:1), we soon find ourselves walking with people, serving, and loving them without needing to fix them, judge them, or control them.

When Jesus told his disciples he'd be leaving them to return to heaven, he also promised that he wouldn't be abandoning them but would send them a *parakletos* (John 14:16, 26; 15:26; and 16:7) or their helper, counselor, advocate. The literal meaning, of this kind of helper, is someone who "comes alongside." Jesus was referencing the coming of the Holy Spirit, who is of course also a perfect representation of Father God as a member of the Trinity. But the description is a reminder that being a Helper often means just coming alongside others and "keeping pace" with them.

As an awkward, shy, pimple-faced kid with a mullet and zero sense of dressing style, I would have had no academic confidence in my teens if not for having Mr. Wagner as my junior-high English teacher. Mr. Wagner "kept pace" with me at a time when I had low expectations of my own academic abilities. To that point, I'd rarely applied myself to school assignments, tests, or essays.

One of Mr. Wagner's teaching methods was having his students journal their personal reflections for each chapter of the current novel being read in class. At the end of every week, we were required to hand in our journals for Mr. Wagner to read. I will never forget Mr. Wagner telling the class that following Monday, "I was reading your journals over the weekend, amazed at the insight you all carry. Let me read one brilliant entry about chapter five that brings up an insight I never noticed in all my years of teaching!"

As he read, I could feel my face flush red. He was reading my journal! When he finished, he flashed me a glance. "The student who wrote this entry should be proud of himself. Amazingly brilliant!"

At his words, a blast of hope ignited in my stomach, plumes of wonder rising to the edges of my mind. Could he really mean what he'd said? It turned out he did. This occurred several more times, eventually drawing me to regularly stay after school to chat with Mr. Wagner for hours at a time. Mr. Wagner "kept pace" with me by demonstrating curiosity and acceptance. By reveling in my ideas. By meaningful, challenging questions that inspired me to grow.

The honor, camaraderie, and affirmation I received from him took effect so that by the end of the year, all my grades improved along with a new determination and confidence to apply myself to studies and life. In short, Mr. Wagner was a Helper.

Our Father is the master at "keeping pace." He never gets tired or weary of our shortcomings. He doesn't have an agenda of control or ulterior motives. He doesn't want to use us. He just desires to come alongside his children, to build camaraderie and work together. As Jesus told his disciples:

> Don't be afraid, little flock. For it gives your Father great happiness to give you the Kingdom. (Luke 12:32)

Our Father is the master at "keeping pace." He never gets tired or weary of our shortcomings.

It isn't about our effort. We sometimes hear people proclaim, "God used me to encourage that person!" Or "I pray God uses me at work." While I understand the sentiment, I don't believe God "uses" his children. Can you imagine if a mother introduced her eight-year-old daughter to friends by announcing, "This is Amanda. She is useful to me for house cleaning"?

On the contrary, Father God wants to partner with you because he is proud of you. When you walk down the street, laugh the way you do, or share your heart in your unique way, he smiles with great joy. "Hey look, that's my child! I love it when he/she does that. It reminds me of us! I'm so proud!"

After all, why do you think the Bible speaks of a great cloud of witnesses watching us run our race (Hebrews 12:1-2)? Our Father is watching over us, cheering us on, and training us for his work. And as our Dad, he wants to walk with us and work together with us even when we don't deserve him. That's called grace!

I remember vividly as a teenager on a missions trip to Mexico City when my Father God pointed my Dictator orphan shadow toward what it looks like to be his Helper in crisis. It was 1988. Our team of sixty people was distributing Bibles door-to-door in teams of two or three. Because I'd been on a couple past outreaches and had some familiarity speaking Spanish, I was placed as a team leader with two elderly women.

The day we went out together, I was in a funk, tired, and insecure. As the youngest person by far on this team, I desperately wanted to feel significant and valued among the adult group members. One of the two women, in her seventies, tried to reach out to me. "Oh son, it's so wonderful someone your age is wanting to serve God. But you've still got a lot of life ahead of you. You'll have seen a whole lot more by the time you get to my age."

Or something like that. She was being kind, but my internal reaction was furious. *How dare she say that! What does she know? Doesn't she think God can use young people like me? She's just jealous and resentful of being led by a teenager!*

Because I wasn't looking to Father God to meet my needs for belonging and significance, I'd slipped into misperceiving her comments as disrespectful. Which in turn inflamed my stubborn resentment. Brimming with irritation, I slid into Dictator mode as I led the two women through our assigned neighborhood. At each door, I waved the ladies forward, directing them to do the talking while I inwardly nitpicked everything they said and did.

The two sweet ladies didn't react but instead reflected my Father by lovingly walking alongside me, serving and encouraging me. We came to the last house. I again coldly stood behind the others, ushering them to take the lead. An elderly woman answered the door, inviting us inside.

What followed breaks my heart with my Father's love. Once inside, my two companions shared the gospel, resulting in an entire family of eight receiving Jesus as Savior. I should have been overjoyed, right? Wrong! I was grumbling inside at their success. Bottom line, I couldn't be happy because Dictator shadows dominated. Sounds like Jonah, doesn't it?

Then our elderly hostess took us into a back room where an old man was sitting in a wheelchair by the window. He hadn't walked for over twenty years. I didn't care. I stood rigidly by the man without a drop of compassion. Then just as we bowed our heads to pray, one of my companions gently took my hand, placing it on the old man's chest. Right when my hand touched his chest, a beautiful instrumental song called St. Elmo's Fire came on over the radio.

At that moment, the anger in my heart crashed into God's love. Tears filled my eyes and dripped down my cheeks as I prayed a fragmented prayer. God's holy presence was in the room. Sunlight from outside flickered through the window, pushing the Dictator shadows away.

Then some of the family members in the room cried out in wonder as the old man began to move his legs. Within minutes, in an audience of tear-stained faces, the old man was walking and praising God. Not only had Father God healed broken legs, but he had healed my heart broken by shadows of control. I was deeply humbled. Despite my ugly attitude, God had honored me by inviting me to partner with him.

That's our Father God, our Helper! Our drive for control may lead us into habitual striving, constant judgment, or impulses to fix others. But our heavenly Dad is still there honoring, loving, and calling us to an adventure, to a partnership, with him. No matter how many times we fall into Dictator tendencies, he'll continue to remind us they aren't who we really are as his child.

REFLECTIONS

- The Helper Impact brings understanding, encouragement, and support.

- Subtle lies from our childhood can distort our abilities to be who we are in Christ as his helper to those around us.

- Our ability to see ourselves, situations, and other people clearly is directly affected by how secure we feel.

QUESTIONS TO CONSIDER

- Which Helper characteristic have you seen most often in your life?

- What does partnering with Father God look like in your life?

- Which primal needs, if met by your Father, would make it easier to be a Helper?

CONNECTING WITH MY FATHER

May I invite you to join me in praying the following prayer.

"Father God, you are my greatest help in life. I invite you into those places where I have tried to meet my needs on my own. I invite you to show me any lies from my past I have believed about who I was or how I should relate to difficult things. I am tired of trying to manage you, myself, and my world. I can't do it! Please show me how you feel about me. I just want to enter your stillness sitting on your lap, Dad. Please come! In Jesus' name, amen!"

CHAPTER ELEVEN

The Loner

I need you, and you need me. Historical research confirms that cultures where there is mutual cooperation thrive. But in modern times, we have largely lost awareness of our need for others. With social media, we have more communication tools but less connection. One relationship guru, Jay Shetty, has marveled that we've been all the way to the moon and back but still struggle to cross the street and start a conversation with a neighbor.

Today's world offers an illusion that we can live independently of others. But God designed our need for belonging to be met within families. When Father God created the first man, Adam, he noted that it wasn't good for man to be alone, so he created Eve out of Adam's rib, forming the first family (Genesis 2:18-24). In the Psalms, we are reminded that God "sets the lonely in families" (Psalm 68:6).

Prolonged isolation can negatively affect every part of our being. Under the mandated social distancing/isolation of the 2020 global coronavirus pandemic, symptoms of depression tripled. Chronically lonely people have tested at higher risk for elevated blood pressure, insomnia, infection rates, heart disease, and dementia. While it is good to engage in purposeful solitude to recharge and refocus, it is not healthy to live as a loner, insulated and isolated from other people.

...the Loner's only way to deal with fear and shame is to isolate themselves from others in overt or subtle ways.

Which brings me to our next orphan mindset—the Loner. Just to be clear, this mindset has nothing to do with being temperamentally shy or an introvert. God created both introverts and extroverts because our world needs both. An introvert by nature, I was shy and withdrawn growing up. But I soon recognized extroverts received more praise, so I yearned to become more extroverted.

During adolescence, my confidence grew in how God had created me. As high school co-president, leader in my youth group, and popular among my friends, I learned to love people and myself. I learned to recharge my introverted side by taking long walks alone, leaving noisy, crowded parties early, or spending extended periods of time in satisfying solitude.

But another reason for my withdrawing manifested especially during times of crisis. As with my other needs, I didn't know how to meaningfully invite Father God into my need for belonging. Over time, sitting in the "orphan shadow" of Loner became comfortable, which in turn led to negative habits and knee-jerk responses. I found it easier to simply avoid people I disagreed with. I judged people I didn't understand and internally raised my own opinions, ideas, and giftings over those of others.

A Loner lifestyle may feel comfortable. But it isn't glorifying to God and does not release the Father's best for our lives. Just as with the Dictator, the Loner mindset is a default way of thinking and living to help meet our primal needs. When the need for belonging isn't met by our Father God at a heart level, the Loner's only way to deal with fear and shame is to isolate themselves from others in overt or subtle ways. Common characteristics of the Loner include:

- **Distrustful**: Unable to trust others due to only seeing others' weaknesses and shortcomings.

- **Independent isolation**: Choosing to live cut off from others/God at a heart level by dictating life on our own terms.

- **Unforgiveness:** Reacting to or withdrawing from others in hurtful ways to show that we are bigger, stronger, and better than others.

- **Living without vision**: Living in the moment without a view of who we are to God, self, and others in light of eternity.

- **Devaluing others:** Not understanding the value of others to our Father's heart, dishonoring and disrespecting others.

- **Self-centered:** Viewing Father God's gifts, calling, and people as tools for our own self-fulfilment and gratification.

- **Non-committal:** Unable to join others due to lacking relational security.

When the Soviet Union collapsed in 1989, the outside world learned of the harsh reality of orphan life in Eastern European nations such as Romania, Poland, and Bulgaria. Orphanages were grossly understaffed. Children were left in their cribs day and night with no contact except for diaper changes and feedings. Research revealed that neglect had permanently stunted these children's brain development, resulting in shrunken gray matter, decreased intelligence, and inability to cope socially with others. In extreme cases, institutionalized orphans rocked themselves for hours, beat their heads with their fists, even bit their own hands to meet their physiological need for touch and healthy social stimulation.

When a child doesn't receive regular caring touch, interaction, and affection, the damaging effects can last throughout an orphan's life. In the same way, when we deprive ourselves of daily communion with our loving heavenly Dad, the results are devastating. We automatically slip into Loner default thoughts and actions. Just like the neglected orphan slaps and punches themselves or others, we do equivalently hurtful things to ourselves or others.

It is impossible for Loners to completely trust another person. The mentality of an orphan who has been responsible for their own survival is: "I've got to take care of myself because no one else will." Believers struggling with this orphan mindset unconsciously push people away, sometimes because they've been hurt in the past, but often because they simply lack experience of our heavenly Father's care.

Have you ever been at some crowded party or church gathering when you spot someone across the room that in your perception hurt you or someone you love? From enjoying conversation and fellowship, your full awareness shifts to center on that person. Uneasy, scared, or angry emotions well up. If you haven't found security and love in your heavenly Father's presence, then like the neglected orphan, you may feel compelled to reactions that harm yourself and others.

For the Loner, this may simply mean avoiding and ignoring that person in self-protection. It may also mean being nice, saying hi, and pretending everything is fine while stuffing down resentment and concealing judgment. When stress, pain, crisis, or uncertainty hits us, the question becomes whether we grab for our heavenly Father's hand for belonging and comfort or hide under that Loner orphan shadow.

Loneliness, insecurity, anxiety, defensiveness, and suspicion plague us all in different situations and in different ways. But what if you could walk into a place where you truly felt at home regardless of the emotional swirl around you? As heaven's adopted child, you were invited into a meaningful, shame-free daily existence with your perfect Father. When you enjoy him, these orphan shadows literally drift out of sight.

BEST SUPERPOWER

If you were dropped into the Middle East about 1100 B.C. and could have one superpower, what power would you choose? Would you want laser-shooting eyes? Invisibility? The ability to outrun any beast? What superpower would have been most valuable three thousand years ago?

The time period I'm referencing was the early centuries of the nation of Israel before they had a king, a historical account we find in the Old Testament book of Judges. Life in ancient Israel was not easy. There was no electricity, mechanization, or hydraulics. This meant growing crops, building houses or roads, digging wells for drinking and irrigation, forging metal into tools or weapons all had to be done by hand. Dangerous wild animals were a constant threat, not to mention marauding bandits and invading enemy tribes. In this challenging world, what kind of superpower would you want to possess?

Without a doubt, I'd pick unlimited strength. We tend to forget in our era of tech nerds pounding on keyboards that everything in the ancient world from gathering food or building shelter to defending from enemies required human strength and endurance. Like the mythological Hercules, the stronger you were, the greater advantage you held.

The Bible actually describes such a man by the name of Samson living in the nation of Israel during this time period (Judges 13-16). Can you imagine what it might do to someone's character if they knew they had unlimited physical strength? In Judges 13, God reveals to Samson's mother before he is born that Samson has been set apart to deliver Israel from the enemy nation that was oppressing them.

As sign of Samson's special status, he was to keep a Nazirite vow (Numbers 6), which included not drinking wine or other fermented drink, not cutting his hair, and having no contact with dead things. So long as Samson kept that vow, God blessed Samson with supernatural strength. But though physically the strongest man in history, Samson was emotionally and spiritually weak. His Loner tendencies eventually led to his defeat in six critical heart battles, cutting short his life and the impact he could have had for God.

DEFEAT #1: SELF AS CENTER

Samson's Loner orphan shadows became apparent when he reached the age to find a wife. Despite his parents' objections, Samson insisted on choosing a wife from Israel's enemies, the Philistines (Judges 14:1-4). When that ended in disaster (Judges 14:10-20), he went on to pursue relationships with prostitutes and other women of ill character (Judges 16:1, 4). One can only wonder how Samson's life might have turned out had he married and remained faithful to an Israelite woman with a heart for God. But as a Loner, Samson seems unable to listen to his parents or anyone else with his best interests in mind. He thinks only of his own gratification, which eventually cuts short his influence as a deliverer for Israel.

The first mention of Samson's supernatural strength comes when he is attacked by a lion on the way to his wedding and rips the beast apart with his bare hands (Judges 14:5-6). Later on, Samson finds that bees have built a hive inside the carcass. Disregarding his Nazirite vow that prohibits touching "unclean" things, including dead corpses, Samson scoops out some honey and eats it. This act demonstrates that Samson's commitment is to his own needs and desires, not the Father God who gave him super-strength. As Loners, we can become vulnerable to making decisions and finding nourishment in places that jeopardize our influence, possibly cutting short the life-giving adventures our Father God has for us.

DEFEAT #2: REACTION AND REVENGE

There is a God-given desire in the human heart for justice to be served. This reflects who our Father God is—a God of both love and justice. But the restless spiritual orphan isn't capable of trusting God to measure out justice in a loving way. For this reason, they will seek to mete out their own justice, sometimes at incredible cost to themselves. Stories of seeking revenge like the *Count of Monte Cristo*, *Hamlet*, or *True Grit* may make for blood-pumping entertainment. But in real life, such actions never bring long-term satisfaction and peace. Why? Because they epitomize the broken, desperate, self-seeking quest for justice on their own terms.

Samson was judge over Israel for twenty years (Judges 15:20). Even though he won many temporary tit-for-tat battles with Israel's enemies, he lacked the self-control and wisdom to ever fully free his people from the Philistines. You can't free others when you yourself are bound.

> Without wise input and unique perspective from others, self-control gives way to reactivity and vindictiveness.

After the disaster of marrying a Philistine woman who betrayed him (Judges 14), Samson finally returns to his in-laws only to discover that his bride has been given to his best man (Judges 14:20). As revenge, Samson collects three hundred foxes, pairs them with burning torches, then releases them to set fire to Philistine grain and vineyards (Judges 15:3-5). The Philistines respond by killing his bride and her family (Judges 15:6), so Samson reacts again by attacking and killing many more Philistines (Judge 15:7). This cycle continues with Samson winning short-term battles due to his God-given super-strength but never pushing the Philistines out of Israel.

Our Father never designed us for isolation. If we are operating independently from others, even with a powerful gift, we are vulnerable. Without wise input and unique perspective from others, self-control gives way to reactivity and vindictiveness. As a Loner, Samson was never able to fully harness his God-given strength and its mobilization potential. In contrast, as we will see later, King David never had Samson's super-strength, yet he conquered far more territory, established more stability, and left a legacy that lasted for generations.

DEFEAT #3: DISTRUST AND SUSPICION

You might say to me at this point, "Hey, David, Samson is winning battles against the enemy! Isn't that good?"

The problem is that Samson wasn't using his gifts to serve God's people but to serve himself. For any of the orphan shadows, our God-given gifts will never become fully developed if they become a means to serve ourselves. We can build bigger churches, ministries, businesses, and careers. But if people around us aren't empowered, then our gifts are not reaching the potential for which Father God designed them.

Just consider the accomplishments of King David who ruled Israel for forty years. As a youth, he killed a giant (1 Samuel 17). Years later, he united the tribes of Israel (2 Samuel 5:1-10). He established Israel's first national capital (2 Samuel 5:6-8; 1 Chronicles 11:4-6), defeated Israel's surrounding enemies, wrote much of the book of Psalms, and was called by God a man after his own heart (Acts 13:22). But many of these accomplishments wouldn't have been possible if David hadn't inspired trust and released the gifts of others around him. In fact, the Bible lists David's thirty mightiest warriors (2 Samuel 23:8-39), demonstrating that David's leadership encouraged and provided opportunities for his colleagues and subordinates to excel.

Jesus gives us an even better example of such leadership. During his public ministry, he healed thousands of sick people, cast out demons, raised the dead, walked on water, and multiplied food. Yet in the midst of performing such amazing miracles, Jesus called twelve disciples to follow him (Matthew 4:18-22), continuously taught them despite their immaturities (Matthew 13:1-9; Luke 9:55; 11:1-13), and sent them out to do the same miraculous wonders he was doing (Mark 6:7-13; Luke 10:1-23). Just before he returned to heaven, he commissioned his followers to go out and change the world (Matthew 28:16-20), encouraging them that they would do even greater things than he'd done in his own ministry (John 14:12). He never made his mission about his own gifts and power but instilled trust and hope in those closest to him by serving and loving them perfectly (John 13:1-17), encouraging them to do likewise.

This is in complete contrast to Samson. Samson's own countrymen were terrified of him. After the Philistines sent an army to attack him, three thousand armed Israelites gathered to confront him. Seems like a lot of men to talk to a fellow countryman! But their conversation reflects the lack of trust and loyalty between Samson and his own people.

> "What are you doing to us?" they demanded of him. "Don't you realize that the Philistines are our rulers?" But Samson replied, "I only paid them back for what they did to me." "We have come to capture you and take you to the Philistines," the men of Judah told him. "All right," Samson said, "but promise me that you won't kill me yourselves." "No," they replied, "we won't do that." (Judges 15:11-14, TLB)

Imagine if Samson hadn't made his battles with the Philistines about his own personal feuds. If he'd demonstrated a vision bigger than his own life, maybe giving his hometown team a Braveheart-like pep talk: "Guys, you're right! These people have been ruling over us for too long, hurting our wives and children. I can kill at least a thousand of them today, and together the three thousand of us can push these Philistines out for good. We can accomplish together more than anyone of us can accomplish alone. I'll fight for you till my last breath. What do you say? Let's fight and destroy our enemies together!"

Instead, his reputation among his own people had sunk so low that his biggest concern was that they didn't kill him before the Philistines got the chance.

DEFEAT #4: INDEPENDENT ISOLATION

As Loners, we don't have the Father's security to mutually open our lives to others. In isolation is where we are most vulnerable. We may seem to be doing well functioning at arms-length from family members, colleagues, even spouses. But if our motivation is not inspired by our Father's love, we are stumbling in orphan shadows. This leads to a constant striving to demonstrate why we don't need others, which in turn results in seeking alliances and comfort from the wrong sources.

Consider Samson seeking comfort in the arms of a Philistine prostitute who lives in the capital city of Israel's enemies. When they try to ambush him, he pulls off an amazing act of strength by tearing off the city gates and carrying them up to the top of a hill outside the Israelite city of Hebron (Judges 16:1-3). Depending on size, whether wooden or covered with bronze, these gates could have weighed up to several tons. Take that, Mr. Universe!

No doubt the enemy would have been intimated by this act. But what about his own people? Imagine awakening to see your enemy's gates on a hill opposite to your town. Surely this should embolden them to fight. But again, Samson's strength is only used to point to himself. He could lift heavy things but was not able to lift and mobilize his own people to accomplish something great.

The problem with Loners is that they focus on themselves to the exclusion of seeing other people's potential. When we see only what we are accomplishing and what others are not, we start living the lie that our ability, opinions, money, or gifting is enough on its own. Only the Father's love can draw us out of this dangerous place.

DEFEAT #5: NO FAMILY PROTECTION

When we receive Jesus into our lives, we join a heavenly family (Romans 9:8). This is not some obscure theological concept with no relationship to our minute-to-minute existence. This family reality has tangible life consequences for all of us right now. God's family is functioning and operates through love and honor (Romans 12:10).

If we attend a small group or church service but our hearts are critical, cold, and angry, we've already embraced an orphan mindset. If we pull back from relationships out of judgment, hurt, or fear, we are slipping into an orphan existence. Living in God's family is more than a one-time encounter but a lifestyle that requires regular mentoring and encouragement from Father God. The consequences of living without this lifestyle will catch up to us in big and small ways.

Samson's lifelong commitment to Loner behaviours caught up to him in a final way through his romantic relationship with Delilah, a beautiful Philistine woman who secretly worked for his enemies (Judges 16:4-21). She repeatedly nagged Samson to prove his love by revealing the secret of his super-strength. Three times he brushed her off with a lie. Three times her true intentions to capture him were exposed. And three times he easily fought off his attackers.

This final episode of Loner living shows that Samson was comfortably sleeping and flirting with a person who didn't really know who he was. The truth was that Samson had forgotten who he was, what his mission was, where he came from, as well as the source of his strength. This is a classic consequence of a Loner mindset. Loners are isolated from their own spiritual family who can testify as to their true identity. When we forget who we are in God, we are truly lost. In the end, Samson loses everything—his strength, his freedom, and his influence.

DEFEAT #6: NO VISION

The final outcome of Loner living is personal imprisonment, despair, and a lack of vision. It isn't enough to know *about* God as your Father. You need to relate intimately *with* God as your personal Dad. Not only will this satisfy the deepest parts of your being, but it will protect you from the mire of orphan consequences.

Tired of Delilah's nagging, Samson finally reveals the true secret of his strength. I.e., that if his hair, uncut since birth due to his Nazarite vow, were cut off, he'd become as weak as any other man (Judges 16:15-17). What followed next must have been traumatic for a man who'd never known what it meant to be subdued, bullied, or defeated. While Samson is sleeping, the Philistines cut off his hair. His strength gone, he is imprisoned, blinded, and set to slave labor for his enemies. The tragedy was that his Loner living left him permanently exiled from his family and countrymen. In the same way, when we lean on orphan Loner shadows, we fall into silent captivity, lacking a vision of who we are and what our purpose and significance is.

Thankfully, that wasn't the end of Samson's story. With all strength and influence stripped away, Samson cried out to his heavenly Father. As his hair grew during captivity, his strength also returned. When the Philistines brought him out to make mockery of their defeated, blind enemy, God answered Samson's prayer, giving him super-strength one last time to destroy more of Israel's enemies than in all his battles to date (Judges 16:22-31).

Samson isn't the only Loner orphan story in the Bible. Some Bible characters exhibit lifetime patterns of a particular orphan mindset while others may display a single incident of that weakness. The Old Testament prophet Elijah is an example of demonstrating Loner tendencies in one specific incident. Elijah had a powerful ministry under two apostate Israelite kings (1 Kings 17-19; 2 Kings 1-2), including a public display of fire from heaven, ending a three-year famine, killing four hundred-fifty false prophets, and outrunning horses.

Then came his Loner moment when Jezebel, queen of Israel, threatens his life (1 Kings 19:1-2). Despite all the powerful supernatural displays, Elijah's isolation catches up to him, leaving him fleeing in fear and sheer exhaustion, despairing of life, and complaining to God that he is the only faithful believer left in Israel (1 Kings 19:1-4). Walking without Father God leaves us vulnerable to view crisis in self-centered ways, leading us to feelings of victimization and/or superiority.

In Elijah's moment of weakness, God patiently encourages him, provides him with sustenance and rest, assures him that there are seven thousand other believers, then ends his ministry isolation by providing a partner, Elisha, to come alongside him and train as his successor (I Kings 19:15-21). While both Samson and Elijah accomplished great things, it was because God worked around their orphan insecurities to bring glory to his name. Today our Father God is walking alongside us, intimately looking to meet our every need so that orphan shadows do not have to rule our lives and legacies.

REFLECTIONS

- Loner orphan shadows selfishly strive to thrive in isolation and distrust based only around their own perceptions, abilities, or experiences.

- Not experiencing Father God's heart meant Samson lived a vengeful, self-centered life devoid of meaningful relationships based around God's mission.

- Having a Loner mindset means that although we may be doing good things in our lives, we are doing them out of self-reliance, self-protection, and self-centeredness rather than a heart for Father God and others.

QUESTIONS TO CONSIDER

- What successes or failures in your life need to be re-positioned with Father God at the center?

- Have orphan shadows of independent attitudes, selfish living, unforgiveness, or reactive choices been your default in any of your relationships?

- What do you believe about yourself and God in these areas?

CONNECTING WITH MY FATHER

May I invite you to join me in praying the following prayer.

"Father God, I believe you never meant for me to live alone. Regardless of my choices in life, thank you, Dad, for never leaving or forsaking me (Hebrews 13:5). I am tired of walking around in circles without your vision for my life. I invite you into those areas

I have tried to maintain on my own. As your kid, I submit all my needs to you. Please show me how you see the family into which you adopted me. Thank you for your love. In Jesus's name, amen!"

CHAPTER TWELVE

The Reconciler

*B*ill Wither's 1972 song "Lean on Me" highlights how we all need a community surrounding us, caring for us, and believing in us. In our busy, disconnected world, how do we slow down and really care for others? Relating daily to God as our Dad causes our hearts to naturally soften. In this place, hurt can't stick to us. We come to know a security that outweighs our pain. In this place, we move toward people because we see relationships as a conduit of healing rather than a liability or threat. Relationships open tangible opportunities for giving his love to others.

I call this Impact Driver the Reconciler. The Bible states that through Jesus Christ we are both reconciled to God and given the ministry of reconciliation (2 Corinthians 5:18-20). Reconciliation means coming together through healing, forgiveness, justice, and love. Being a reconciler means taking a stand in the midst of relational discord, tension, and conflict to offer peace, encourage discussion, and bring people together. Common characteristics of the Reconciler Impact Driver include the following:

- **Clarity seeker:** Feeling secure in our Father's view of us helps us forgive others' weaknesses so we can explore their perspectives and celebrate their potential and gifts.

- **Catalyst:** Living with Father God empowers us to approach conflict with an open heart to bless and bring together people of differing opinions, ethnicities, and experiences.

- **Hope-bringer:** Feeling the Father's joy for us enlarges our heart, allowing us to experience delight in connection and invite others to view each other through our Father's eyes.

- **We-focused:** Living every moment with a view of who we are together as Father God's family brings energy to our relationships, enabling us to see the power of unity in diversity.

- **Open-hearted:** We overflow with respect and honor for others because we can see the value the Father places on others.

- **Joyful loyalty:** In spite of relational disappointments or shortcomings, we are enabled to embrace people as the Father's children with specific gifts to enjoy, encourage, and serve.

- **Committed:** We are able to commit to others because our relational security comes from the Father alone.

When we are personally impacted by our heavenly Dad, we begin to enjoy people as his children and as brothers and sisters in the larger human family. We develop "eyes" to see what makes them so special to our Father (Ephesians 1:17-18). We may still see their weaknesses or remember the pain they've caused. But as we allow Father God to share his love with us, we experience a shift in perspective about others. It may be immediate or more gradual, but in the end we find ourselves enjoying, cheering, and supporting those who have been in conflict with us or with those around us. Our hearts are filled with Father God's ability to act as a bridge between those in conflict, network people from opposite sides, and encourage those who feel hurt and alone.

FROM LONER TO RECONCILER

God glorifies himself by taking our weakness and transforming it to reflect his goodness. How? Through a Dad's relationship with his children. Jesus's entire earthly mission was to reconcile us to himself (Colossians 1:19-20). After receiving Jesus as our Savior, we received a new nature, *his* nature (2 Corinthians 5:17; Ephesians 4:22-24), which includes being a Reconciler. You may feel stuck in Loner ways of reacting to relationship pressures. But you and I spiritually carry Jesus's DNA of reconciliation (2 Corinthians 5:11-21).

> God glorifies himself by taking our weakness and transforming it to reflect his goodness.

My own journey out of a Loner mindset is rather historic. I confess that I've reveled in Loner behaviours and attitudes in my past. A variety of things can draw us into Loner patterns. For some, it may be a vow to not be hurt again. For others, a lifestyle of self-reliance. For others, a dishonoring attitude that shuts down relationship.

But for me, it has always been fear. I was just seven years old when the terror of isolation was first imprinted on my little heart. My friend Clayton had invited me to his birthday sleepover. I'd never been away from my parents overnight and had no clue what lay ahead. After the cake, games, and plenty of fun activities, the other boys drifted off to sleep.

But in the quiet darkness of a home not my own, my own seven-year-old heart raced with terror. I desperately missed my mom and wanted to return to familiar, safe smells and sights. I spent most of the night huddled wide-awake in my blanket, at times going into the washroom to cry. I survived till morning, but as I returned home, I recognized something I'd been ignorant of to this point in my life. I was suddenly aware how alone we all are regardless of how many friends or family surround us.

Funny how one innocent sleepover can introduce insecurity and encourage fear. Over the following years, my underlying orphan perception that we are all ultimately vulnerable, weak, and isolated in our struggles continued to grow. As a pastor's kid (PK), I watched church conflict destroy committed relationships between congregants. I saw small groups disintegrate into gossip and division over unresolved hurts. As church leaders, my parents were intimately involved in toxic relational situations. Seeing the pain, betrayal and misunderstanding they encountered, I worried for their safety and well-being.

As this Loner awareness grew in me, I developed strategies to meet my own core needs for protection and belonging. It was easy to pull away when things looked unsafe or when I could get hurt. As I moved into my adolescent years, there were times when I broke away from people, even friends, to cover up my insecurities, never truly sharing my fears. How incredibly lonely this is but also agonizingly boring. Isolation has a way of killing creativity and wonder. When we live in an isolation based out of fear, we are unable to play.

I eventually grew up and got married, but even marriage to an incredible woman was impacted by knee-jerk Loner reactions. During difficult times or when feelings of insecurity overwhelmed me, I automatically clammed up into my shell. My Loner mindset could falsely justify my habitual withdrawing, unforgiveness, and critical analyzing of my wife. You can guess this didn't help grow trust in our relationship!

Many of us feel that because a response comes naturally or automatically, it must be who we are. This is an orphan lie. That said, things do have a way of catching up to us. I've already shared how my Loner mindset reached a crisis when my beloved church community misperceived what I was called to be for them. In the final months before my life-changing encounter with Father God, I would park my vehicle blocks away from my church office, sneaking in through the back door so as not to encounter anyone. Forget about curiosity, exploring, or playing! Orphan shadows will strangle those delightful natural qualities of a happy child, leaving you bored, armored-up, and missing the adventure your heavenly Dad has for you.

PLAYING WITH FATHER GOD

After the counselling sessions and Father God encounter I shared earlier, I drove back to my in-law's home in central California, reuniting with my daughters and wife. We stayed for another week before flying back to Canada. It was during this week that Father God showed me how he loves to playfully surprise me.

Hockey is a pretty big deal in the snowy white north. So it likely won't surprise you how much I enjoyed watching and playing hockey. The biggest prize in the National Hockey League (NHL) is the Stanley Cup, much like winning the Super Bowl in American football. If a team wins the championship, they get to bring the

Stanley Cup to their city to celebrate. Sometimes the Stanley Cup is put on display in public places. Fans will spend hours in line to get their picture taken with the Stanley Cup. Unless, of course, you have connections!

Earlier that year, Boston's NHL team, the Bruins, had won the Stanley Cup. I was glancing through my in-laws' local newspaper when I noticed the Boston Bruins were bringing the Stanley Cup to a California resort just a couple hours away for public viewing. Seeing my interest, my sweet mother-in-law decided we should have a field trip to take in this iconic Canadian symbol.

We'd packed up lunches and were preparing to leave when we called the resort, only to learn that the public viewing out had already taken place. Since we were already packed up, we headed out anyway, figuring we could at least enjoy a hike. We'd just driven into the resort parking lot when to my astonishment I spotted two men in black tuxedos and black gloves carefully hoisting a four-foot silver statue across the parking lot. It was the Stanley Cup!

As the men disappeared into the resort, I jumped out of my in-laws' van and raced after the two gentlemen. I followed them into the lobby of the hotel restaurant, where the men carefully placed the Stanley Cup on a small circular table. Introducing myself, I learned that the Bruins team owners had decided to bring the Cup out unannounced for a few hours. I was stunned at the timing. For the next hour, I had an uninterrupted "date" with this special icon, touching it, lifting it over my head, taking every kind of picture one could imagine. Amazingly, there were no lines, wait, or competition to see this incredible prize!

Watching the setting sun as we drove back to my in-laws' home, I felt awe, exhilaration, and the same deep peace I'd experienced with the two counselors a few days earlier. Tears filled my eyes as it hit home that Father God really was my Dad, and like any loving earthly father he really did want to play with me and surprise me in ways that mattered to me. I sensed his warm presence wrapping around me and his loving voice saying, *David, this is just the beginning of how I want to surprise you as your Father.*

And that was just the beginning! Back home in Canada, my world exploded with security as I invited God to be my own personal Father. I was no longer trying to avoid anyone at the office, gas station, or family gatherings. Though our church situation was still chaotic, I was able to smile and even be playful. How was this possible?

> You can't be playful without being one hundred percent present in the moment.

Learning to play is about learning what it means to be Father God's son or daughter. Science has shown the benefits of play to our social and mental development, whether sports, music, chess, or imagination games. How much more is it true for us as spiritual beings? Your heavenly Dad is delighted to give you spiritual gifts and talents (1 Corinthians 12:7-11; Romans 12:3-8). He wants to help you unwrap them and discover what it means to play (John 14:26).

You can't be playful without being one hundred percent present in the moment. As fathers or mothers, how often do we get preoccupied by our to-do list, a book, or watching TV while our son or daughter is trying to share something with us. The beautiful thing is that our real Dad, Father God, never gets distracted. He is always one hundred percent attentive to us one hundred percent of the time.

When we truly accept this as reality, what powerful security this builds in a human heart! This realization was transformative for me personally and affected my own fathering. In 2012, I experienced a dream where my oldest daughter was looking up into my eyes with delight and openness. I could see her with 3-D clarity. Then in my dream, Father God asked me, *What's the most valuable thing you can give your daughter?*

In my spiritual piety, I thought I knew the answer. I needed to lead and train her to follow God. But even as the answer tumbled from my mouth, I knew I was wrong. What was I missing?

I watched the answer unfold in my dream. To my horror, I saw myself engaging with my daughter, only half-present, distracted, anxious, and annoyed. These emotions were like a gust of tainted wind blowing down on my little girl's heart, leaving her unconsciously polluted by me. Worse yet, I could see this interaction did not empower her nor our relationship.

Then my Father God's voice gently countered, *The most valuable thing you can offer your daughter is your presence. Giving your total self to her builds a bridge for you to be able to invest effectively in her all the other things you want her to know and be. Without a healthy heart connection, you've got nothing.*

I woke up somewhat stunned but recognizing Father God is my greatest example of being a parent. When I reach out to him, he is always present, available, and focused on me. He may not answer my questions the way I want him to or when I want him to, but his love and affection are unquestionably present. He is omnipresent, revealing himself to Moses thousands of years ago as "I am that I am" (Exodus 3:14), not "I will be when I will be."

After that personal epiphany, I realized how much I wasn't present with people close to me, especially my family. You can't have a relationship with a distant, detached person. I could use justifications like busyness, unexpected stress, or just the way life is in the twenty-first century. But using those excuses for family doesn't cut it.

I felt an urgency to see change, so I set myself a goal to be completely present in the moment with my family and friends, living in a heart-state of love. Twenty days passed, and I felt like I'd failed. Being consistently present seemed impossible. In fact, the more I tried, the less I attained my goal. Disillusionment set in. I woke up at 4:00 a.m., tossing and turning. Sitting alone on my couch, I cried out, "God, what's the matter? Why can't I do this?"

Silence. My thoughts drifted back to my adolescent years when I would sit for hours captivated with God, tears flowing down my cheeks, feeling his love. I was struck by how present God felt to me back then. Why was it so different now? I pleaded, "God, please touch me with your love!"

More silence. I felt empty, full of doubt, ready to get up and try my pillow again. Then I sensed an inner tugging for my attention. *Wait, David, just wait!* After several minutes, I felt a touch and heard Father God's voice washing over me. *I love you, David. Let me touch your heart.*

Tears streamed down my cheeks as God's love poured over my dry heart. Waves of acceptance, affirmation, and deep care washed over me continuously for close to an hour. It was so awesome to feel my Father God chuckling playfully with me and enjoying me just being me. It was then I knew what being present in the moment was supposed to look and feel like. Father Dad was feeding my starving heart, filling me with a deep sense that I belonged, that I was protected, that he was caring for all my needs, and that my life was purposeful in his eyes.

The next day my wife left for a weekend trip to visit her family. I was left with our daughters, who were then two, four, and six years old. Let's just say I had no grand expectations. But to my surprise, despite nasty diapers, girls fighting over dolls, nightmares at 3:00 a.m., and unexpected demands from my work, I was totally and effortlessly present in the moment with my girls, full of love and enjoyment of their big or small quirks.

In short, I was playful. I discovered that the secret to being present isn't mental gymnastics, a mountain of determination, better scheduling, or less stress. These things aren't bad. But the true key to being present is a soft heart. By soft heart, I mean a state of interacting with Father God's gentleness in real time. Letting that gentleness and love affect our state of being to such a degree that we care for people as we have been cared for.

We can only give what we have received. To pursue Father God believing he will affect my ability to playfully enjoy others seems too simplistic or perhaps mystical. But believe me, when dirty diapers, screaming little girls, and every other demand imaginable is calling for my attention, simplistic sounds good!

REFLECTIONS

- The Reconciler Impact Driver brings people together by being committed and celebrating with an open heart people's uniqueness regardless of differing backgrounds, positions, and opinions.

- Letting Father God touch our past memories and/or perceptions transforms our ability to be playful and present in all relationships.

- Experiencing the healing power of Father God's ever-present presence creates space in me to be present with others at a deeper level.

QUESTIONS TO CONSIDER

- Where do you see opportunities to be God's Reconciler?

- What does Father God being "playful" with you look like in your life?

- For this Impact Driver to grow, what primal needs must Father God meet?

CONNECTING WITH MY FATHER

May I invite you to join me in praying the following prayer.

"Father God, I believe you are present and happy with me every moment. Thank you for the relationships and people you have placed in my life. I invite you to show me how you see me in these relationships. Because you are with me, I am fully secure and safe. I say yes to engaging my world with you. Thank you for your joy. In Jesus's name, amen!"

CHAPTER THIRTEEN

The Slave

Slavery has been one of the most common miseries of the human race since Adam and Eve became orphans. For thousands of years, millions of men, women, and children on every continent and from every ethnic background have been traded and treated like property. A slave's labor, body, and personhood are exploited through threat of physical, mental, and emotional punishment by an oppressive master.

Over recent centuries, most nations have officially abolished slavery. Yet unofficial debt labor, sex slavery, child slavery, and domestic servitude still persist like a festering infection. Global slavery is estimated to encompass tens of millions of human beings across much of the planet. But I would suggest that number should be in the billions. Slaves work in high rises, banks, and schools. They lead Sunday School classes and large ministries, companies and governments. They fill every corner of society.

How is this possible? Simply put, the Slave is another "orphan shadow" mindset we can unknowingly flip on autopilot, leaning into it for direction and support. This mindset is marked by bondage, addiction, obligation, and/or driven performance. It has nothing to do with your temperamental bent, personality, or lack of spiritual experiences. I've known powerful, influential leaders caught in a Slave mindset. Nor is it solely being bound to porn, alcohol, drugs, food, or some other addiction. It is a default way we respond to life and people when we are not drawing from our Father God's comfort and hearing his voice.

The truth is that most orphan mindset Slaves look pretty good on the outside. We go to work, pay our taxes, take our kids to Little League games, and volunteer at church. We may feel fairly content most of the time. But if we allow ourselves to walk through the inner rooms of our heart, we'd be surprised how empty and dim some of them are. Still, what's the big deal if a few areas of our heart are dark or dusty?

As a thirteen-year-old in 1986, I traveled with a group from Canada on my first mission trip to Mexico. It was my first experience living in a castle, or at least that's how I remember it. After a couple days of gas stops, dusty roads, and overnighting at churches in sleeping bags, our bus arrived at a luxurious fenced estate. My eyes widened at the trimmed hedges, beautiful gardens, even a heart-shaped pool. A majestic building topped by a round glass spire rose several stories into the sky. If this was our lodging, count me in for a missionary calling!

We learned that the estate and building was built as a wedding gift from a wealthy aristocrat to his beautiful fiancée. When she died tragically just days before their wedding, the heartbroken groom deeded the entire estate to a local church. Now used as a

Christian retreat center, the estate had space to host several outreach teams simultaneously.

Sounds awesome, right? But over the following week of ministry into the city, my "castle awe" faded. Eating, sleeping, sweeping, mopping, and mundane daily living in this grand palace was very different from admiring its majesty at a distance. While it would make a great museum with its huge, echoing salons, winding turret staircase, and elegant fixings, it didn't feel like a home.

Just hours before his arrest, Jesus shared with his disciples that he and Father God wanted to make their "home" in those who believed and received him (John 14:23). The Bible calls our bodies God's temple (1 Corinthians 3:16-17; 6:19-20; 12:27). While Father God's presence resides in our body, he also longs to take up residence in the specific inner rooms of our personhood so that he can bring us the warmth of his light, enjoyment, and love. These different rooms may be marked entertainment, career, ambition, finances, friends, and other compartmentalized parts of our life.

> God doesn't force himself into the different rooms of our hearts.

God doesn't force himself into the different rooms of our hearts. He waits patiently until we begin opening these closed-off places to him, room by room. What a tragedy it is when we feel we must strive and stress to scrub squeaky-clean the exterior of our "temple" while leaving our loving heavenly Dad waiting in the lobby of our souls.

Before inviting Jesus to be our Lord and Savior, we were all slaves to sin (John 8:34; Romans 6:19-20). Once we are redeemed through placing our faith in Jesus, the Bible says we've been set free from sin (John 8:36; Romans 6:18, 22). But in actual experience, whether in our own life or others, we still find ourselves slaves to sinful behaviour. What is going on?

It goes back to our prior discussion in chapter six of the difference between our spiritual *position* as God's child and our heart *condition* in relation to our heavenly Dad. Our Father has redeemed us from sin through his Son, not through our own striving, determination, or performance. But if we haven't yet known the heart reality of a sweet daily reliance on Father God, if we aren't finding our core identity in our heavenly Dad rather than our own performance, we naturally slide into a Slave mentality, striving to make our lives a beautiful presentation on the outside while entire heart "rooms" are hollow and trapped in forced servitude.

For one person, a Slave mindset may involve trying to earn praise and approval. For another, it may be striving for career or business success. Yet another may be dealing with secret addictions. But in each of these mentalities, an obligation to serve and perform for ourselves or someone else has become a default way of living. Or it may involve quiet surrender, i.e., accepting and living in the shadows of forgotten disappointment and heartbreak. Characteristics of the Slave mindset include the following.

- **Idolizing others:** Finding value and personal fulfillment in things/tasks/people outside of who we are as God's child.

- **Hopelessness and insecurity:** Living without knowing the Father's joyful "yes" for our personhood in every situation.

- **Subservience and compliance:** Cowardice and compulsion to come under people and systems that are dominating.

- **Mismanaging inheritance:** Lacking a stewardship mindset to believe, plan, choose, and act on managing a heavenly inheritance.

- **Putting God in a box:** Living formula-driven, caring more about performance than the Father's voice.

- **Defensiveness:** Compulsively self-protecting our own efforts, abilities, and performance.

- **Feeling unworthy:** Living without a sense of being valued, priceless, and delighted in by Father God.

- **Lacking voice:** Lacking authority because our definition of ourselves has not come from what our Father says about us.

The era of legalized American slavery was destructive, crippling families and destroying millions of lives. After the American Civil war ended in 1865, comments from freed slaves give a glimpse into slavery's devastation. One freed slave, John Fields of Lafayette, Indiana, commented starkly:

> It was the law that if a white man was caught trying to educate a Negro slave, he was liable to prosecution entailing a fine of fifty dollars and a jail sentence . . . Our ignorance was the greatest hold the South had on us. We knew we could run away, but what then?

The sad reality of the Slave identity is that we sabotage our own peace, success, and joy. Why? Because to a slave, freedom has no meaning. There is no mentor, coach, or guide on how to use freedom wisely. Living in bondage also means we don't learn to take responsibility for ourselves since a slave doesn't exercise free will. As Steve Arterburn, founder of New Life Ministries, notes in his book *Regret-Free Living*: "The more responsibility you take for your choices, the less regret they're likely to cause you."

Regret can be a signal of past times when we weren't living reliant on our Father. If we are being drawn back into a Slave mindset, we will be attracted to rules because they give us an excuse not to take responsibility in making decisions (Galatians 4:1-7). When things go wrong in our lives, how tempting it is to blame the devil or even God with such excuses as "oh, well, I guess it wasn't God's will after all!" Or "the enemy deceived me!"

When under pressure or in crisis, the Slave identity feels powerless and helpless. Why? Because a slave isn't a son or daughter but a possession no different in position or value than a mule or milk cow. In the eyes of their oppressors, the enslaved person has no inherent value or voice like a child does to a loving Father, but only the service and labour they provide. If they can no longer perform profitably, they have no worth. Another former slave, Fountain Hughes of Baltimore, Maryland expressed this forcefully:

> If I thought, had any idea, that I'd ever be a slave again, I'd take a gun an' jus' end it all right away. Because you're nothing but a dog. You're not a thing but a dog.

How debasing slavery is to the human soul. For the mindset of Slave, the lie is that our value lies only in what we can perform. When we find our security in anything else other than our Father God—rules, our own gifts and performance, a spiritual leader we idolize, our career or business successes, we trade in our true positional identity as the King of king's sons and daughters for the false, deceptive identity of a parentless, valueless Slave.

BARTERING TO LOSE

Sadly, when we choose to live with an orphan Slave identity in any area of our lives, we take on shackles that bind us as cruelly and painfully as the shackles many slaves once wore. We find the biography of one such orphan in the Old Testament book of Judges. Jephthah was a warrior and judge who led Israel for six years around 1150 B.C. As during Samson's era, Israel had strayed from God, which led to domination and tyranny by a foreign oppressor. Jephthah was called by God to free Israel (Judges 11-12). But as we'll learn from his story, his inner battles proved tougher than the outward ones.

SHACKLE #1: UNWORTHINESS

Hurdling the spear in the hot sun, Jephthah watched with pride as the glinting blade sliced through the air, splitting the tied sheath of straw down the middle. The crowd cheered. This son of Gilead's founding father had just won every category in the annual games. But fury twisted the faces of his watching half-brothers.

The oldest stepped forward, calling out, "Brothers, let him smirk as much as he wants. We know who he is and who we are. We are the legitimate sons of our father Gilead. He is but the son of a whore."

Turning to Jephthah, he looked his burly, perspiring half-brother up and down with a sneer. "If you think you are going to share in our inheritance just because we share a father, think again! You may consider yourself a great warrior because you can handle a spear and sword. But you are still the son of a prostitute. My brothers and I have made our decision. You'll leave our birthplace, our home, our town now!"

Jephthah had already recovered his spear. Raising it, he sneered, "Or what? Do you want to fight me? Do you really think you can win?" His cold glare swept across the angry faces of his other half-brothers. "Do *any* of you think you can take me on?"

A loud crack was followed by pain shooting through Jephthah's right shoulder. As he fell back, the next stone hit him in the side of the head. As a barrage followed, his oldest brother called out, "Maybe none of us can fight you. But you can't fight all of us either! We are the true and rightful heirs of our father Gilead! You have no inheritance here! Now that our father is gone to his ancestors and isn't here to protect his bastard child, you do not belong here. In fact, you never did. Go peacefully, and we'll let you live!"

Bruised and bleeding, Jephthah limped away. Not one of Gilead's town elders who had just been cheering his prowess raised a hand or voice to keep him from leaving. Grabbing his weapons and the belongings he could carry, Jephthah threw himself into the saddle of his horse and galloped out of town. He had no idea where he was going. But he had no intention of ever returning.

This is the introduction we have to a warrior leader called Jephthah (Judges 11:1-3). The son of the tribal leader for whom the town was named and a local prostitute, he was cast out by his legitimate half-brothers and rejected by his community. Moving to another region, Jephthah became leader of a gang of outlaws and earned a reputation as a fierce warrior.

Though a leader, Jephthah carried a deep sense of unworthiness as might be expected when treated as an illegitimate orphan and driven out with no more resources or support than a slave would have. In consequence, he chose to turn his gifts as a warrior and leader to raiding and scavenging the countryside (Judges 11:3).

We've all experienced rejection, pain, and disappointment at some time. A Slave mindset takes root in those memories, those rooms in our heart that haven't experienced Father God's loving acceptance. I am blessed to be the father of four daughters, and I love affirming my daughters in their identity. When I speak words of affirmation and acceptance over them, their eyes light up with delight and their little faces can hardly contain their big smiles.

What is happening? As their father, I am meeting their designed needs for belonging and significance. How much more should we need our heavenly Dad's parenting? As a son or daughter, we have a created, inbuilt hunger to know our Dad's acceptance and affirmation. Without those, we will put our gifts to scavenging and pillaging rather than God-honoring purposes.

> As a son or daughter, we have a created, inbuilt hunger to know our Dad's acceptance and affirmation.

SHACKLE #2: PUTTING GOD IN A BOX

Fast-forward Jephthah's story, and we see the elders of Gilead traveling to recruit Jephthah as their leader. They've been attacked by the Ammonites, an oppressive enemy, and now they are in need of Jephthah's warrior skills to defend the town. Understandably, Jephthah needs some convincing. After all, these elders (who very likely even included some of his half-brothers!) aren't approaching him because they now realize they were wrong in their past attitudes or because they suddenly like, honor, or respect Jephthah. He is still the illegitimate son. They would hardly be inviting him back home if all was peaceful and prosperous.

Have you ever been asked for help by someone who doesn't respect you? I certainly have. Most of the time, it makes me want to show that person I'm deserving of their acceptance. In this case, Jephthah finally did accept their offer (Judges 11:4-11). He now has the chance to earn the acceptance, honor, and respect he desperately wants from his own people by delivering a complete and lasting victory.

How we handle high-stake situations reveals whether we are living in orphanhood or anchored in the Father's heart. Trust me, in these moments of crisis, we will operate the way we've actually lived over a lifetime, not according to what Sunday School has taught us should be the correct biblical response. Though Jephthah is now an outwardly-powerful leader, the chink in his armor remains: his deep, unfulfilled need for belonging, acceptance, provision, and protection. As both a spiritual and earthly orphan, Jephthah does not know God as Father, leaving him operating with a Slave mindset.

Jephthah's feeling of helplessness is revealed in his desperate attempt to barter with God. A common practice among generals and kings in the ancient world was to make a vow to their gods in exchange for victory. Though the Spirit of the Lord had already come upon Jephthah, (Judges 11:29) guaranteeing a great victory, his ingrained belief of unworthiness and helplessness leads him to make a terrible vow.

> And Jephthah made a vow to the LORD. HE SAID, "IF YOU GIVE ME VICTORY OVER THE AMMONITES, I will give to the Lord whatever comes out of my house to meet me when I return in triumph. I will sacrifice it as a burnt offering. (Judges 11:30-31)

An orphan Slave hasn't encountered Father God's goodness, love, and parental desire to protect and provide for his children.

So they unconsciously believe they must strive, earn, and perform to acquire God's blessing. The result is trying to put God into our own box, relating to him as orphans on our terms. Formula-driven conversations are the result where we attempt to exchange our goodness, possessions, or resources for his favor.

SHACKLE #3: MISMANAGING INHERITANCE

Slaves, living spiritually orphaned, don't have an inheritance reality. Inheritance is a family word. It is the passing on of property or wealth at death. It also is the passing on of a name, traits, and characteristics at birth. Since they are in bondage, orphan Slaves toil for someone else. Never having worked alongside their Father to create and build up an inheritance, they will naturally squander what they do not understand. Jephthah's great chasm of emotional need leads to his inheritance trickling through his fingers.

> When Jephthah returned to his home... who should come out to meet him but his daughter, dancing to the sound of timbrels! She was an only child. Except for her, he had neither son nor daughter. When he saw her, he tore his clothes and cried, "Oh no, my daughter! You have brought me down and I am devastated. I have made a vow to the LORD THAT I CANNOT BREAK." (Judges 11:34-35)

A Slave mindset means we do not understand grace. It means that we must rely on our own efforts, formulas, and exchanges with God. It means slipping into carnal-spiritual accounting. How good have I been lately? How much have I been praying for breakthrough? How much have I sacrificed for God lately? All these efforts prevent us from grasping and living in the inheritance Father God has freely given us.

As God's son or daughter, you have an inheritance of heavenly proportions. Do you know what that is? Have you learned to walk in it by walking with him, or have you lived a life of formulas, exchanges, and performance?

SHACKLE #4: HURTING THOSE AROUND US

In the end, Jephthah lost his only child, the one who could carry on his lineage after he passed away. Though human sacrifice was unlawful in Israel (Deuteronomy 18:10) and clearly a sin, the Bible indicates that Jephthah carried out his misguided orphan shadow (Judges 11:38-39). I have no doubt God would have released Jephthah from his unlawful vow, but Jephthah's orphan view of God would not permit an acceptance of such a gift of grace.

A Slave mindset of performing for our perceived victories hurts our families, our friends, our communities, and even ourselves. Whether habitually working overtime versus spending time with our kids or maintaining a dutiful volunteer record at church to earn praise from someone we respect, performance inevitably leaves us empty. It also leaves those around us disillusioned as they realize they are less important to us than our performance.

An added bondage of the Slave mindset is that we must defend and maintain what we've earned by our own efforts. We find our worth from what we accomplish rather than what our Father shares with us. So when our accomplishments are challenged, we become offended and attack. This was true in Jephthah's life. After being challenged by another tribe in Israel, Jephthah reacts violently.

Then Jephthah, furious at the taunt of Ephraim that the men of Gilead were mere outcasts and the scum of the earth, mobilized his army and attacked . . . So forty-two thousand people of Ephraim died there at that time. (Judges 12:4-6, TLB)

How costly it is to try to fix our feelings of unworthiness. In Jephthah's case, it cost forty-two thousand of his own countrymen. The same is true today. Some of the most offended people in the world are Christians. Though we are brothers and sisters in God's family, how easily we divide and attack each other. Only the Father can unite his family, and only when we know him can we stop trying to defend ourselves.

The Bible is filled with orphan Slave mindsets. Another such example is Aaron, Moses's brother and spokesperson (Exodus 7:1) and Israel's first high priest (Exodus 28-29). Though Aaron served God faithfully for many years, his Slave tendencies led him to became subservient to other people in their sin. After Moses had been absent an extended period of time on Mount Sinai receiving God's law, the Israelites demanded that Aaron build them an idol (Exodus 32:1). Caring more about what others thought than God, Aaron built a golden calf for Israel to worship, causing many to sin (Exodus 32:2-6).

On other occasions, Aaron went along with Miriam in her sinful jealousy of Moses (Numbers 12) and with Moses in his sinful disobedience of striking the rock when God told him to speak to it (Numbers 20). Similarly, if we carry a Slave orphan shadow in any room in our heart, we tolerate attitudes of unworthiness, resulting in offense, obligation, helplessness, a loss of inheritance, and pain to those around us. Only our heavenly Dad can fill our heart with dignity to help us view every area of our life through his love.

REFLECTIONS

- Slave orphan shadows slide toward self-bondage through a trustless, performance-driven focus of obligating myself to my abilities or others' abilities.

- Without experiencing the dignity sonship provides, Jephthah lived trapped in formulaic negotiations with God; despite his striving, he ultimately suffered more loss than gain.

- Having an orphan Slave mindset means we are compelled to perform and strive for an inheritance we have already received in Christ.

QUESTIONS TO CONSIDER

- In what areas of my life do I feel I can make myself worthy through my own efforts?

- What relationships or situations cause me to bend subserviently or live obligatorily?

- What do I believe about myself and God in these areas?

CONNECTING WITH MY FATHER

May I invite you to join me in praying the following prayer.

"Father God, my heart is amazed that you call me your son/daughter. I can't comprehend fully this love that cares for every detail of my life, including how many hairs are on my head. Thank you for the dignity and worth you give me freely as your child. Please teach me how to step out of the shadows of performing for belonging, provision, protection, and significance. I welcome your love to disrupt me. In Jesus' name, amen!"

CHAPTER FOURTEEN

The Advocate

Our world is crumbling under the heavy weight of centuries of accumulated social cannibalism. Racial injustice. Gender injustice. Economic injustice. Ethnic injustice. The list goes on and on. Our cities, neighborhoods, and workplaces are marked by the influences of envy, hatred, lust, and greed. How do we as Christ-followers relate to the frenzied conflict, angry debates, and accusations?

Jesus was the world's first real Advocate (1 John 2:1). Without being hooked by the arguments and accusations of the people of his day, Jesus stepped forward with influence, sharing security, rest, and love to the broken. American pastor and author Rick Warren writes, "The purpose of influence is to speak up for those who have no influence." Because you are in Christ, you have that same influence. But where is it?

Leaning into God as your Father gives you the security to be able to see with compassion the small, weak, and marginalized all around you. It will also fill you with boldness to stand up for others. When your identity is grounded in being cherished as Father God's son or daughter, this gives you a voice to step out and speak up, freeing others to move beyond the confines of social shaming, personal addictions, image management, or some other form of obligation-living in an attempt to gain acceptance. Common characteristics of the Advocate Impact Driver include the following:

- **Stands with the helpless:** Gives compassion and support to those who are vulnerable or unaccepted.

- **Problem-solver:** Finding value and personal fulfillment in our Father's heart frees us to open our minds to new possibilities in every situation.

- **Imaginative:** Knowing the Father's joyful "yes" for our personhood frees us to dream with God and bring hope to the hopeless.

- **Experimenting:** Living under the Father's authority frees us to risk, experiment, and explore God's gift in us and encourage it in others.

- **Proactive:** As God's child, we carry a stewardship mindset to believe, plan, choose, and act on managing an endless heavenly inheritance.

- **Challenging the process:** As God's child, we don't conform to a formula-driven performance but instead yield to a lifestyle of responding to the Father's voice.

- **Feeling worthy:** Experiencing that we are unconditionally valued, priceless, and delighted in by Father God frees us from compulsive behaviour, self-protecting, and legalistic striving to be acceptable.

- **Voice:** Living under Father God's authority frees us to risk, speak out, and declare truth.

Subtle signs of Slave shadows showed up early in my life. I've already mentioned being extremely sensitive and insecure as a child. In fact, I was sensitive about being sensitive! When I first comprehended God's grace as a ten-year-old, it was powerful. But because I'd never really interacted with the Author of grace, I couldn't completely grasp it at an emotional level.

These Slave tendencies came to a climax when I was twenty-one, revealing the inadequacy of my grasp on who God was. At this point, I was still single, living with my parents, and working at a computer store. As mentioned before, over just a few months I got into a car accident, saw a business start-up fail, and had a relationship crumble, all at the same time our church was going through its own crisis.

Since I truly loved God, I didn't realize my identity had become based around what I could accomplish for him versus experiencing who I was as God's son. I'd been a spiritual leader in our church since early adolescence, leading youth groups, worship, missions teams, etc. I'd even helped lead our church's unity float ministry, participating in parades across Canada with a $100,000 decorated float, live worship band, dozens of singers, dancers, and flaggers, all publicly singing declarations of praises to God.

I was unaware of how much I'd placed my security in church leaders and my own formula for success and spirituality until our church went through its period of conflict, which included the disbanding of the float ministry and many church members leaving.

My misplaced faith in church leadership and my own ministry influence was shaken to the core. Feeling exposed and humiliated, I crashed into deep depression and hopelessness, wondering where God was in all this.

The truth was, he was always there. Because a Slave mindset lives from the *outside-in* instead of the *inside-out* where Father God dwells, I was not empowered to see him. But occasional small cracks in my hardened heart let in my Father's love. One such time came after returning home from a late-night concert. My heart heavy, I retreated to my bedroom, where I began weeping unrestrainedly.

"God, please help me!" I cried out desperately. "I can't live like this."

Right then, I felt Father God's love pouring into my heart. His tender acceptance and affirmation of who I was broke me. After several more minutes of weeping, I felt God impressing on my mind an image of a baby being born in a tent in the jungle. It seemed as though the baby's birth was inconvenient, and I felt the baby's spirit take on self-hatred. I identified with that baby, crying out for God to heal my own heart of self-hatred. Needless to say, I had quite the crying session that night!

A few days later, my dad asked me out for breakfast. Toward the end of our meal, I casually mentioned the image I'd received of a baby's birth in a jungle tent and my tearful reaction. To my astonishment, my dad told me he was the baby born in that tent and had struggled with self-hatred throughout his life, tracing it back to his inconvenient birth.

My dad's parents were part of a sizeable group of Canadian Mennonites who'd immigrated to Paraguay during the first half of the twentieth century. Selling everything, they'd moved from

Manitoba to the Paraguayan jungle to start a farm from scratch. The living situation turned out to be dire, and my dad's mother had given birth to him in a tent in the middle of the jungle during the rainy season. She'd neither wanted a child under such desperate circumstances nor felt connected to him during the early formative years of his life.

As we talked, my dad shared how these experiences had planted seeds of unworthiness in his heart. Years later after connecting with God as my Father, I recognized it was he who had been reaching through time and space to heal wounds of self-hatred passed on through my earthly family line. As with Jephthah, our Slave mindsets can affect our children and their children in turn. I am so glad our Father sent his Son to stop orphan living. And I am in awe that he pursued me as his son. However, until we make room for him in our hearts, the insecurity of fatherless living continues. I wish I had known this growing up.

> I recognized it was he who had been reaching through time and space to heal wounds of self-hatred passed on through my family line.

FROM SLAVE TO ADVOCATE

Slaves have no rights, so there is no voice to speak out for the weak or underprivileged. The Slave mindset tells us to just keep our head down and follow the rules. We feel powerless to bring change. But when our inheritance is secure with Father God, we are freed to stand for others. This is the story of Christianity through the ages. The early church cared for dying people abandoned by their relatives during plagues and epidemics. Throughout the centuries, Christians on every continent established hospitals, orphanages, and schools to lift up the poor and politically-discarded peoples. Was this always done perfectly?

No. But no other group in history has been as active to advocate for the weak and broken.

After my own life-transforming encounter with God as my Father in 2011, my heart became increasingly open to standing up for marginalized people. It has been my privilege especially to open doors for younger people and encourage others to listen to them. One such time occurred in 2015 when my family and I were serving in an orphanage mission station in Mexico. As an ordained minister, I'd been asked to preach. But first, a group of homeless street boys had been invited to give a three-minute testimony.

This particular gang of boys, who slept on the beach, had been experiencing an incredible touch from God to the point that they themselves were witnessing and praying with strangers. Ten minutes passed, then fifteen, while the boys continued to share a powerful, exuberant testimony of God's goodness. The audience began grumbling that they were taking time from the speaker (me!) with some even calling for the young men to sit down. I quickly stepped up and quieted the crowd, encouraging them to not miss what God was sharing through these young men.

What a difference a little time with our Father can make. In earlier years as a young, ambitious pastor without a daily connection with my heavenly Father, I would undoubtedly have taken offense myself that such insensitive, presuming young men were abusing my speaking time. Now my heart was in a different place. Being fully secure in my Father's acceptance, value, and purpose for my life freed me to accord significance and belonging in turn to these marginalized boys, using my voice to advocate for them at the risk of being misunderstood.

Our Father, his Son Jesus Christ, and his Holy Spirit (i.e., the Trinity) are the ultimate Advocates (John 14:16, 26; 1 John 2:1-2).

Spending time with our heavenly Dad shifts our hearts to live who we already are in Jesus without the motivation of performing for acceptance.

PIVOTING AROUND A SAFE CENTER

Sometimes in life our sense of direction meanders without purpose or focus. Sometimes we are clouded with confusion, blocked by barriers we do not understand. Because of our core need for significance in order to have a purpose and meaningful existence, this can be hard. Other times we feel alone, disconnected, and unworthy, stuck in relationships we don't want, wondering if we will ever feel alive.

In these times, we need someone safe who walks alongside us, gently probing our motivations, helping us find our sense of purpose. *Pivoting* references something being able to turn, like on a hinge, while staying secure at its center or core. When we are receiving heavenly security from Father God, he becomes our center, and we are able to *pivot* or turn in the best, healthy direction without losing who we really are. If we will just open the door and give Father God a chance, we will be surprised by how many "rooms" of our heart need freedom, and how he gently shifts us toward freedom and meaningful purpose.

As mentioned before, in 2013, I felt Father God releasing me from the church, where I was a pastor, to start my own consulting company. Its focus was to serve organizations and leaders with consulting, training, and executive coaching. My newly-growing relationship with Father God was changing how I processed decisions and dealt with relationships. But I was about to get a chance to move out of the Slave mindset to the Advocate mindset.

One of my first client organizations was in the technology industry. This company had been growing quickly with about forty employees and no human resource manager. I'd been called in to do an organizational review and help managers develop their people skills. After a couple months working with the CEO and his managers, I was seeing a lot of positive changes.

I'll never forget the Friday afternoon this CEO called me to a meeting with himself, the company's pragmatic lead manager and one of their programmers, a hard-working, middle-aged woman. The CEO explained that there'd been a situation, then invited the lead manager to elaborate. Monotonously, the manager read a statement detailing how this female programmer had for the third time broken a piece of software.

Throughout his reading, the programmer shifted awkwardly in her seat and shook her head. Once the statement was read, she dove into defending her position, her face strained and voice shaky. Meanwhile, the manager repeated angrily, "You keep breaking things! It's costing us big time! It's your fault!"

> When we are receiving heavenly security from Father God...we are able to pivot ...in the best, healthy direction without losing who we really are.

By the end, the programmer was asked to leave work early with pay for the day. Once she left the room, the manager started in emphatically, "She's got to go! None of my team like her. She doesn't listen at all!"

After some discussion, the CEO turned to me. "David, we need to fire her. Can you write up the paperwork and email it to me by Monday morning?"

I nodded uncomfortably, a little dazed that a decision had been reached this quickly. Something seemed off, but since I was new to organizational development consulting, I felt uncertain. As

I drove home, I took a step back to consider the situation without other people's strong voices trying to sell an idea. I suspected this programmer was not being fairly treated, and writing up dismissal papers would be the wrong direction. From what I knew of the managers, a process for effectively communicating her past mistakes didn't exist. Nor was there any commitment to train or support employees.

As I walked in the front door, my daughters burst into song, happily welcoming me home. My wife, Svea, was away visiting her sister, so the girls and I were planning a daddy-daughter weekend. I threw a frozen pizza in the oven. While it baked, I shot an email to the company CEO, explaining my belief that firing the programmer would a mistake. My heart sank when he shot back a reply that he'd already contacted the company lawyer and one reason they'd engaged my services was to do these types of things.

After supper, the girls and I piled onto the sofa. As we watched a Winnie the Pooh movie, I tried to sort my confused thoughts. What could I do? As a new company, I couldn't afford to lose this client. And of course, they had the right to fire whoever they wanted-ed. As a consultant, I just gave advice, so it wasn't on me if they chose to do something I didn't agree with.

As the movie ended and I put the girls to bed, I battled Slave orphan shadows in my thinking. My core needs for provision, belonging, significance, and protection would be threatened if I lost this client organization. In similar situations, hopelessness had led me to pull back on using my voice to challenge others. My habitual response was to be subservient and go along with everyone else, so as to be accepted and make things work.

I cried out to Father God about the situation and eventually fell asleep. The next morning, I was awakened by my seven-year-old second daughter. Diving onto my bed, she wrapped the covers around her. "Hey, Daddy, let's play!"

Still trying to wake up, I stalled with a question. "Oh, honey, it's a bit early to play. Did you have any dreams last night?"

She nodded matter-of-factly. "Of course, Daddy! I dreamed about you last night."

When I asked her to share her dream, she continued, "I dreamed you went to a red-brick building to help the people there. A dark-haired man met you at the front door. He said you were right and that he wanted to do the things you'd told him to do. Then you were really happy. Can we play now, Daddy?"

I was struck with wonder at her dream. I'd never taken my daughters to this location nor mentioned my consulting crisis the previous evening. And yet, her description had many parallels to my dilemma. The software company worked in a red-brick building. The CEO had dark hair. I knew in that moment I had the power to advocate for this programmer even if it meant losing my client. As my daughter scampered off, I breathed a prayer. *Father, I trust you.*

On Monday morning, I drove to the red-brick building, curious to see what would happen. What unfolded was exactly what my daughter had dreamed. Meeting me at the front door, the CEO shared that over the weekend he'd an uneasy feeling about firing the programmer. Over the next half-hour, a new plan to help train her came together. I was beyond elated.

When we let God be our Father, he will help us reflect who he is to the world. He cares about the details and wants to help us out of orphan shadows that have bound us in the past. Are you feeling hopeless, insecure, or unworthy? Are you tired of working for God's approval or the approval of others? Are there areas of your life—a relationship, situation, habit—where you automatically react subserviently, struggling to find your voice and your freedom? Your Dad has been waiting since the beginning of time to father you.

REFLECTIONS

- The Advocate Impact Driver's motivation is to creatively give hope and a voice to the voiceless through loving, proactive challenges of oppressive traditions, processes, and/or people.

- Relationship with our Father flips our heart's orientation from *outside-in* living to *inside-out* living.

- A healthy turning or shifting of our priorities, focus, or direction occurs when we respond to our Father God's playful, curious, and affirmative pursuit of us as his kids.

QUESTIONS TO CONSIDER

- In what ways have I experienced God advocating for me personally in my life?

- Where are there opportunities for me to advocate for the voiceless, weak, or marginalized in life, neighborhood, or at work?

- When considering any type of pivot, which primal need(s) is demanding more peace?

CONNECTING WITH MY FATHER

May I invite you to join me in praying the following prayer.

"Father God, it is so awesome you enjoy being with me. You are really changing me! I let go of trying to produce peace by striving with things outside of myself. Thank you for your unconditional delight in me. I honor how you gently nudge me in new directions of opportunity and blessing. Please help me to have your heart so I can shift and help those you have placed in my life. In Jesus' name, amen!"

CHAPTER FIFTEEN

The Hoarder

*A*fter a weekend away, Rachel was taken aback by the foul stench emanating from their newly-adopted son's bedroom. It smelled like rotten meat. "Ahmed, honey, do you know why your room is smelling so badly?"

Terror filled Ahmed's eyes. Face twisting in panic, he pulled on Rachel's arm. "Mommy, please, I'm hungry! My tummy hurts. Please, can I have just a little more?"

Puzzled, Rachel knelt down and pulled her new son into her arms. "Sweetie, we just finished supper. You already had five pieces of pizza. I think you can wait until your bedtime snack, honey. Your tummy needs a break. But you haven't answered my question. What is that awful smell?"

Instead of answering, Ahmed pulled away and ran screaming down the hall. Rachel's heart ached as she followed him. She found him huddled under the kitchen table, crying and whimpering. Why was he so afraid? What was he hiding in his room? Had he found some kind of dead animal?

Uneasily, Rachel followed the scent trail back to Ahmed's bedroom. What she discovered confused and horrified her. Piles of food had been stuffed under the bed. Mounds of Cheerios. Pieces of stale bread. Dried-up apples. Even hardened macaroni-and-cheese. The stench of rotting meat turned out to be turkey sandwich meat she'd served over a week ago.

Doesn't he like my cooking? What have I done wrong? Returning to the kitchen, Rachel discovered Ahmed in the act of stuffing his pockets with bananas, mouth jammed full of the yellow fruit. This was the beginning of Rachel's and her husband Arnold's experience with food insecurity, a common obsession for foster and newly-adopted children who've endured a scarcity of sufficient and nutritious food in the past.

When I heard Ahmed's story, Arnold and Rachel had adopted the five-year-old Ethiopian boy just two months earlier. They'd brought their new son into their home with great joy and love in their hearts. But within hours, Rachel had noticed Ahmed's odd and at times disturbing behaviors related to food. When he'd arrived in the United States, Ahmed was below the healthy weight and height range for his age. But he quickly began gaining weight. He constantly guzzled soda, overate at every meal, and begged for more food every hour of the day.

Rachel frequently discovered Ahmed in the kitchen looking through cupboards, refrigerator, and freezer. He expressed his utter amazement at how much food Rachel and Arnold kept in their home. It took many months and much prayer, patience, and reassurance before Ahmed's hoarding tendencies began to fade.

Why is hoarding such a common compulsion for foster or newly-adopted children? Sadly, these children haven't known the security of a loving parent providing for their basic needs. For orphans trapped in this trauma, the natural reaction is to unconsciously protect against scarcity by gathering as much as possible and hoarding it against a time of need.

Ahmed's story is a snapshot of the entire orphan human race. Throughout millennia, people have hoarded because they've never known the ultimate security of a loving Father able and willing to meet their every need. Kings and peasants, elite and workers, poor and rich, all have hoarded to provide for unmet needs, whether those are social, financial, emotional, or spiritual.

Even in church circles, we've propagated hoarding as a spiritual right. We've likely all heard or felt the following sentiment when passing some stoned junky or unemployed homeless person begging for change on a street corner: "Don't give money to those people! Remember, God only helps those who help themselves."

In fact, that sentiment is not in Scripture! The last time I checked, our heavenly Dad helped us precisely when we couldn't help ourselves. I've lived in a major urban metropolis, and I've seen the harsh realities of addiction and homelessness. I am certainly aware of the dangers of enabling wrong behavior through thoughtless handouts. But what then should be our response to the needs of others? Do we know the Father's heart for us? Is his heart for us overflowing from us to others? I would encourage all of us not to answer these questions too lightly.

Like an earthly orphan, the last "orphan shadow" mindset we unknowingly wrap around ourselves for support and security is the Hoarder. Don't assume you are free of this mindset because you don't pile up boxes of useless junk in your attic, garage, or home.

The Hoarder mindset relates less to how much stuff we have and more to where we derive our peace. This orphan shadow leads us to seeing ourselves as the source for provision, usurping our Father's place in our lives.

This shadow is also marked by scheming, comparing ourselves, reckless competition, or even excluding others from a group because we want to hoard relationships for ourselves. As a consultant, I've witnessed managers hoarding staff or resources for their department at the cost of organizational health. The expressions of a Hoarder mentality are endless. But ultimately, it boils down to our default response in meeting both material and non-material needs.

"What's the big deal if a few areas of my life tend toward comparison and scheming?" we may ask ourselves. Such a question reveals we don't have a clue how large, deep, and wide our Father's provision is for us (Romans 8:31-32) or how much Father God just wants to be our Papa or Daddy. Some characteristics of a Hoarder identity include the following.

- **Provision anxiety:** Living with a vacuum of peace when considering present and future needs.

- **Scarcity:** An unconscious way of viewing ourselves regardless of what we actually have.

- **Manipulative:** The tendency to use deception to ensure we are provided for.

- **Scheming:** The default response of planning to get more with our own abilities.

- **Comparison:** The obsessive desire to see if we have more than others in order to alleviate the pain of insecurity.

- **Striving:** Living with a heavy weight that results from trying to earn blessing on our own.

- **Judgmental:** The compulsion to evaluate others in order to assess if we need more.

- **Win-lose mindset:** A view that any type of resource is limited or feeling threatened when another person receives much with the assumption that we will therefore receive little.

SCHEMING AWAY BLESSINGS

Picture a loving father calling his son and daughter to himself when they turn of age. This father is a king, so he owns many estates, overseeing great wealth and resources. He is also known for his kindness, gentleness, and wisdom and is always available to his kids when they call for him. When his newly-adult son and daughter arrive at the palace, the king invites them to share their hearts. He discusses with them their future responsibilities as his heirs. The son and daughter are both excited with their newfound purposes. At the end, the king reminds his son and daughter that if they need anything at any time, they only need to ask.

The daughter is joyful as she leaves the king's palace, secure in the knowledge that all her needs will be provided for. In contrast, the son's mind is racing with anxiety. Caught up in all his new responsibilities and the resources needed to complete his tasks, he forgets his father's promise of provision. His insecurity grows.

In time, the son comes to resent his sister's joyful, carefree attitude. He becomes increasingly judgmental, comparing himself with his sister, burdened by needs, scheming hopelessly to achieve his father's purpose for his life on his own. Overwhelmed by trying to provide for himself, he eventually distances himself from his father, eyeing him suspiciously, believing the king does not care for him anymore.

Sadly, when we choose to live with a Hoarder mindset in any area of our lives, we find ourselves bound by schemes and deceptions that subtly move us away from our heavenly Father. The Old Testament story of Jacob, whose twelve sons became the twelve tribes of Israel, is a sad example of a Hoarder mentality (Genesis 25-33). Grandson to the great patriarch Abraham and son of Isaac, Jacob had a twin brother named Esau. Though Jacob grew up in a wealthy family with large herds of livestock, his Hoarder mindset negatively influenced his decisions and ability to enjoy God's call on his life.

SCHEME #1: GRABBING FOR STATUS AND WEALTH

Imagine that a prophecy had been pronounced over your grandfather, your father, and yourself before you were even born. This promise from God involved founding a nation that would bless and impact the whole world. You grew up hearing about these amazing promises and the inspiring stories of faith fulfilled in your father's and grandfather's lives. You look around at the vast wealth, blessing, and influence into which you were born.

Shouldn't all this leave you feeling confident, secure, and faith-filled as you move into your own destiny? Sadly, great benefits and prophetic promises didn't guarantee anxiety-free living in Jacob's case. His name actually meant "to be crooked" or "to deal dishonestly." And he lived up to his name!

As already mentioned, Jacob and Esau were twins. But Esau was born first, which in biblical times made him the heir. As heir, the firstborn son inherited a double portion of property, authority, and status (Deuteronomy 21:15, 16). But before the twins were born, their mother Rebekah received a prophecy from God that her younger son would take precedent over his older brother.

> And the Lord told her, "The sons in your womb will become two nations. From the very beginning, the two nations will be rivals. One nation will be stronger than the other; and your older son will serve your younger son." (Genesis 25:23)

As we read on in Jacob's story, we learn that Rebekah favored Jacob over his twin brother, so you can imagine she probably told him the story of how God had prophesied his ascendency over his brother. Add to this that that the twins' father Isaac favored Esau over Jacob. A perfect storm for sibling rivalry.

Jacob knows God has a great future and purpose for him. He's heard the incredible stories of God's miracles and intervention in his father's and grandfather's lives. He's been raised in a home where God is worshipped. So you'd think he would sit back, relax, and look forward to God's prophecies coming true.

Unfortunately, Jacob's orphan Hoarder mindset tells him that he's the one who must make God's prophecy come true. If God destined him to rule over his brother, then he needs to do something to get himself appointed the heir and firstborn instead of his twin. His first scheme involves getting Esau in a moment of weakness to sell his birthright as firstborn to Jacob for a bowl of soup (Genesis 25:29-34).

But of course that wasn't enough since this underhanded deal wasn't exactly endorsed by the twins' father. And there was more to the firstborn's birthright than a two-thirds portion of the estate. The father's blessing on his firstborn would seal his position before God as heir. And since Jacob believes in God and in the power of that firstborn blessing, he sets his sights next on making sure his father's blessing comes to him instead of his twin.

What comes next demonstrates just how dysfunctional this family has become. The Bible passage doesn't tell us if Rebekah communicated to her husband God's prophecy that their older son would serve the younger. Either way, God's promise was hardly conditional on Jacob wheedling the firstborn's blessing from his father. But clearly both Jacob and his mother have the Hoarder mentality that they must intervene for the prophecy to be fulfilled.

By this point, an aging Isaac is almost blind. So when Rebekah learns that her husband is about to bestow his blessing on his firstborn, she helps Jacob pose as his twin. Jacob does trick his father out of his blessing. But it doesn't lead to replacing his twin as firstborn. Instead, Esau is murderously enraged while Jacob ends up having to flee for his life from the land he'd schemed to inherit and take refuge in his mother's homeland with her brother Laban (Genesis 25:29-34; 27:1-46).

Broken relationships, scheming, deception, striving, and a drifting away from our inheritance are typical results of spiritually orphaned hoarding. Because literal orphans have often been cut off from their birth family's inheritance, they may feel compelled to fight for their own legacy, support, and provision. So too as spiritual orphans, we may know God's Word and believe God's promises for our lives, but the emotions bubbling up from how we truly see ourselves, our situation, and our heavenly Dad are what will dictate our response. If our hearts don't know who our Dad is, we will slip into subtly striving to meet our own provision needs so we can fulfill his call on our lives.

Despite Jacob's behavior, we see beautiful glimpses of our heavenly Dad in this story. Even after Jacob has done everything wrong and is fleeing for his life, God sends Jacob a dream filled with promises for his future.

> "I am Jehovah," he [God] said, "the God of Abra-
> ham, and of your father, Isaac. The ground you are
> lying on is yours! I will give it to you and to your de-
> scendants. For you will have descendants as many as
> dust! They will cover the land from east to west and
> from north to south; and all the nations of the earth
> will be blessed through you and your descendants.
> What's more, I am with you, and will protect you
> wherever you go, and will bring you back safely to
> this land; I will be with you constantly until I have
> finished giving you all I am promising." (Genesis
> 28:13-15, TLB)

As a spiritual orphan, Jacob could mentally understand what God was saying, but he clearly was not fully experiencing Father God's message of security because we immediately see him falling into the Hoarder orphan trap of creating his own assurances through manipulation. Instead of his brother or mother or father, this time he tries to manipulate God.

> And Jacob vowed this vow to God: "If God will help
> and protect me on this journey and give me food and
> clothes, and will bring me back safely to my father, then
> I will choose Jehovah as my God! And this memorial
> pillar shall become a place for worship; and I will give
> you back a tenth of everything you give me!" (Genesis
> 28:20-22, TLB)

He is essentially telling his heavenly Father, "I'm not going to trust you until you've proven that you are God. If you do that, I will give you a portion of what I have."

Because insecurity is the foundational nature of being a spiritual orphan, living with a Hoarder identity means that God can never give us enough assurances and promises. We will continually need to scheme, manipulate, and strive with God for provision. This may mean striving to pray more. Or advancing our own vision by promoting our God-given gifts. Or manipulating and negotiating an exchange with God. There is no true rest on the inside.

SCHEME #2: GRABBING FOR SECURITY

When Jacob flees to his uncle Laban, he soon finds he's met his match as far as a Hoarder mentality. For twenty years, Jacob works for Laban, greatly increasing his uncle's wealth and possessions. Laban in turn repeatedly cheats Jacob much as Jacob cheated his brother. Meanwhile, Jacob is still trying to manipulate God through superstitious schemes to tip flock breeding agreements in his favor (Genesis 30:31-41).

Still, God kept his promise to Jacob. Despite Laban's trickery, Jacob became a rich man with four wives, eleven children, servants, and many flocks. By the end, he was beginning to recognize it was God who had blessed him rather than his own efforts (Genesis 31:4-12).

In the midst of Jacob's tense relationship with Laban, God calls Jacob to return to his father's house. This undoubtedly made Jacob a little anxious. Spiritual orphans don't know security. They've never had a father watch over them and be their defense. Once again, Jacob's response is tainted by a Hoarder mindset. Though he obeys God's command, he clearly lacks faith that God will protect him in his obedience, so he once again resorts to his own efforts to ensure God's promises are fulfilled. After twenty years as Laban's son-in-law and business partner, he simply takes off with his wives, children, and flocks and without so much as a word to Laban (Genesis 31:17-21).

Father God to the rescue again! After seven days of hot pursuit, Laban catches up to Jacob, but not before God warns Laban in a dream not to harm Jacob. Living with a Hoarder mentality in any area of our lives, whether provision, anxiety over relationships, stability, or safety, leads us to live in fear, dishonoring others. Have you made bad decisions based on a negative assumption about a relationship or work situation, only to discover that God was working it out all along in the background? I have! Our Father God has us covered all the time in every situation.

SCHEME #3: GRABBING FOR SAFETY

Father God will many times invite us into situations that expose our orphan ways. These may include crisis situations where our way of doing things falls short. In these times, we have an opportunity to come to our senses and return home to our Father.

In returning to his angry brother Esau, Jacob was confronting his past, and from his actions it's clear he is doing so with great fear. Father God reaches out, sending angels to reassure Jacob (Genesis 32:1-2). But Jacob's Hoarder mindset once again leaves him scheming to soften Esau through his own efforts rather than trust God's protection.

> Jacob sent messengers ahead of him to his brother
> Esau in the land of Seir, the country of Edom. He
> instructed them: "This is what you are to say to my
> lord Esau: 'Your servant Jacob says, I have been stay-
> ing with Laban and have remained there till now. I
> have cattle and donkeys, sheep and goats, male and
> female servants. Now I am sending this message to
> my lord, that I may find favor in your eyes.'" (Gene-
> sis 32:3-5, NIV).

When the messengers return, they inform Jacob that his
brother is approaching with an army of four hundred men. Jacob's
Hoarder anxiety immediately explodes through the roof. He immediately resorts to his default mentality—scheming and manipulation. First, he divides his belongings, family, and servants into two
camps, sending one on ahead so that if Esau attacks one, the other
might escape. Wouldn't you like to be one of those in the first group
being sent to a warrior brother with four hundred men?

He then devises a series of gifts to appease the well-deserved
wrath of his warrior brother. He sends waves of livestock at intervals,
instructing the servants herding them to tell Esau these are gifts
from his brother, who is coming along behind. He follows this by
dividing up his wives, children, and remaining herds, placing his
lesser concubines and their children up front, his second wife Leah
and her children next, and his favorite wife Rachel with her son at
the rear in the position of greatest safety if an attack should come
(Genesis 32:7-21; 33:1-3).

So where is Jacob in all this? He stays at the very back of the
line, increasing his own odds of surviving any potential massacre
caused by his own actions. After all, ladies first, right?

When caught by a Hoarder mindset, our value system places ourselves at the center of every decision. Our ability to take responsibility for our mistakes, let alone sacrifice for others, is lost. The more financial, relational, spiritual, or social capital we accumulate through Hoarding behavior, the more we have to resort to fear, anxiety, and scheming to maintain and keep our stuff. Like Jacob, we overlook that our Dad has been there all along, helping us, providing for us, protecting us, and blessing us.

WRESTLING FOR BLESSING

As a child, I loved wrestling with my dad, and he loved romping with me, testing my strength against his, tumbling and rolling on the living room floor. Likewise, Father God meets Jacob alone under the cover of night to wrestle with his boy, pursuing his heart (Genesis 32:22-31). The circumstances are certainly unique. Jacob has sent his household on ahead across the river while he stays behind. We're never told why. Was it to continue his earlier prayers beseeching God's intervention with Esau (Genesis 32:9-12)?

> When caught by a Hoarder mindset, our value system places ourselves at the center of every decision.

We can only hope it wasn't cowardice, placing not only his wives, children, servants, and herds between himself and Esau's army of four hundred men, but a river too! Nor are we told what makes Jacob begin wrestling with a man he encounters. But it's clear Jacob knows this is no ordinary man because after wrestling all night, Jacob tells the man, "I won't let you go unless you bless me" (v. 26).

It's also clear the man could have ended the wrestling match at any time as he then touches Jacob's hip, immediately dislocating it. He then confirms to Jacob that he is actually God in human form when he gives Jacob a new name: "Your name will no longer be Jacob, but Israel because you have struggled with God and with humans and have overcome" (v. 28).

Can you visualize this scene? Jacob has lived with a Hoarder mindset his whole life, leaving him stubborn, not willing to yield. God has been wrestling for Jacob's heart just as long, calling on Jacob to trust his Father's ability to bless him instead of seeking to bring about blessing through his own efforts. Now after an all-night wrestling match, the sky is lightening to dawn. God is done wrestling, as indicated by his disabling of Jacob. Jacob can't so much as stand up on his own two feet, but he still won't give up.

Clutching onto God with all his strength, Jacob finally utters words his Father has waited a lifetime to hear from his boy: "I will not let you go unless you bless me."

After all that has happened, Jacob finally seeks Father God's blessing, recognizing that all his own hoarding efforts have been useless. God did bless Jacob, but he also left him with a limp from that dislocated hip as a permanent reminder that Jacob had wrestled with God face to face, yet God had lovingly, mercifully spared his life (vs. 30).

It is the same for each of us. When we come to the end of ourselves, we will hear God calling us out of orphan living. If we respond, he marks our souls, doing what only a Father can do. He also names us, declaring who we are in him. The new name God gave Jacob—Israel—literally means "God rules" or "God fights." In other words, Jacob no longer needed to provide for himself by scheming, striving, and self-protecting. Yielding to his Father meant that God ruled, that God was in control, that God would fight for his child. So Jacob could simply rest in God's provision.

Your heavenly Dad wants to show you how able and abundant his provision is for you in every area of your life. You are his boy, his girl. If an earthly father like myself can delight in doing things and giving gifts to make my precious daughters happy, imagine how much God delights in providing for his children as Jesus reminded his audience in his Sermon on the Mount.

> So if you sinful people know how to give good gifts
> to your children, how much more will your heavenly
> Father give good gifts to those who ask him. (Mat-
> thew 7:11)

We find plenty of other examples of Hoarder orphan mentality in the Bible. Another such Hoarder was Gehazi, the prophet Elisha's personal assistant. Working under Elisha provided Gehazi with a front row seat to many miraculous demonstrations of God's faithful provision. A barren woman conceiving a child (2 Kings 4:17). A boy raised from the dead (2 Kings 4:35-37). Poisonous soup being purified (2 Kings 4:38-41). Bread being multiplied for a hundred people (2 Kings 4:42-44).

Unfortunately, seeing was not believing for Gehazi because his view of reality was choked with a Hoarder mindset of scarcity. After God healed Naaman, a mighty Syrian commander, of leprosy, Naaman wanted to repay Elisha with gifts (2 Kings 5). Elisha refused the offer. Caught in provision anxiety, Gehazi manipulated a situation behind Elisha's back to collect silver and garments for himself. After lying about his actions, Gehazi is rebuked by Elisha and contracts leprosy himself until his death (2 Kings 5:26-27).

A Hoarder mindset leads to restless living, thinking, and feeling because we can't simply rest in our Father's provision but must be constantly striving, manipulating, and scheming to provide for our own needs. It breaks our Father's heart to see us caught, anxious, and striving for provision when he longs for us to live secure in his rest (Hebrews 4:3-10).

REFLECTIONS

- Hoarder mindsets compare, strive, and scheme for an advantage because they are blinded by the illusion of scarcity.

- Despite Father God's promises of blessing and influence, Jacob's pattern was to grab and scheme for blessings, relationships, and safety until he was forced to cry out to God for help.

- Being caught in a Hoarder mindset means no amount of favor, successes, possessions, or God's promises and blessings can quench the restless need for more.

QUESTIONS TO CONSIDER

- What would you feel if every source of income and physical security you had today evaporated in five minutes?

- How often do you compare your life situation with family members, friends, colleagues, and strangers?

- How much do you include God as your Father in the long-term and short-term planning and acquiring of your needs?

CONNECTING WITH MY FATHER

May I invite you to join me in praying the following prayer.

"Father God, I honor you as the source of all provision in my life. How much I want to know your heart as a Dad to provide for me as your child. I believe there is a great adventure in learning to let you personally provide for my 'daily bread' needs. I let go of comparing, scheming, and striving. I welcome you to show me your heart for all my provision needs. In Jesus's name, amen!"

CHAPTER SIXTEEN

The Giver

Though there is more wealth in our world than at any other time in history, provision anxiety is at an all-time high around the globe. How many times have you worried about some aspect of provision in the last month? Being actively connected with your heavenly Dad grounds your whole being in perfect security. This security comes from knowing our Father is able to perfectly provide for all of our primal needs, setting us free to live and give as he does.

As we do, our Hoarder mindset gives way to that of a Giver. Our normal tendency is to feel good about giving to good causes or deserving people. But our Father defines abundant giving very differently in giving his beloved, perfect only Son for an undeserving world:

Someone might perhaps be willing to die for a person who is especially good. But God showed his great love for us by sending Christ to die for us while we were still sinners. (Romans 5:7b-8)

For this is how God loved the world: He gave his one and only Son, so that everyone who believes in him will not perish but have eternal life. (John 3:16).

Common characteristics of the Giver Impact Driver include the following.

- **Attentive to other people's needs:** Living with an overflow of peace when observing present and future needs of others.

- **Generous:** Relating to our Father gives us an abundance mindset, which affects how we steward resources our heavenly Dad has given us.

- **Resource-secure:** Being a son/daughter means living with an internal wellspring of peace emanating from the awareness that our Father has all our needs perfectly covered.

- **Intentionality:** Living under the covering of a generous Father frees our will to make long-term and short-term decisions out of freedom and peace.

- **Possibility-minded:** Freed from the weight of toiling for our provision, we now look to our Father for clarity on earthly activity assignments.

- **Contentment:** Relating to Father God steadies our hearts to enjoy whatever we have in the moment. We are freed to be content in every situation without needing to compare or evaluate others to assess if we need more.

- **Trusting:** As a child, we enjoy dreaming with our heavenly Dad beyond our current circumstances or situation for the benefit of his purposes.

- **Win-win mindset:** A view that our Father is the originator of all blessings, leading us to feel happiness when someone else receives a bountiful blessing, knowing joyfully that every blessing comes from Father God without favoritism.

PUTTING YOUR EGGS IN ONE BASKET

Like many lower-middle-income families, my family experienced financial pressure. Seeing my parents struggle to pay for dishwasher repairs, necessary bills, and a reliable vehicle filled me with frustration and anxiety. Determined not to live in such stress and scarcity, I vowed to do everything in my power to safeguard myself from poverty. I was extremely frugal with my money. I would make a pair of jeans last twice as long by not washing them.

Still, provision anxiety grew internally. I tried claiming verses on provision as though God was an ATM into which you just had to deposit the right scriptures. These efforts brought me no closer to the security I craved or to knowing Father God's heart to provide for me. I began comparing what others had relative to my own situation. I gradually moved into scheming and striving, planning out businesses and ministries, making sure I didn't leave my eggs all in one basket so that I wouldn't be vulnerable to neediness.

The irony was that I believed God was good and loving. I'd seen him provide many times in different ways, and I believed he wanted to provide for me in every situation. Yet there remained an overarching insecurity when it came to physical/financial provision. I didn't know how to walk intimately with a relational Father-Provider. In consequence, I walked outwardly as a strong Christian leader, quoting scriptures of faith and God's love, while inside I lacked the deep-rooted sense of security and abundance that only comes from dynamic, relational heart exchange with our heavenly Dad.

My journey from an orphan Hoarder to Giver is an example of God's mercy and grace. While I grew up with loving parents and never suffered the extreme deprivation of an orphan like Ahmed, financial uncertainty and a perceived lack of provisional needs became my heart's vulnerability. Viewing my parents' financial struggles through my own immature lens led to self-binding expectations of what I needed to accomplish financially. Thus began a lifestyle of quiet hoarding. Throughout adolescence, I saved every paycheck and was a hesitant, calculated giver. Below the surface was a restless fear of scarcity tied to a constant scheming of how to unlock the next big opportunity for myself.

In the midst of this, Father God kept promising to love me and take care of me, sometimes in pretty obvious, spectacular ways. But no matter how miraculous the provision, it was never enough. Why? I knew I had a Father God, but I didn't know my heavenly Dad in a personal way as a son knows a loving father. Knowing God in this way redefines how we see ourselves and by extension how we relate to every other thing in our lives. As Christian speaker Scott Nary, founder of 420 Fire Ministries, writes:

> There is something about the Father that loves to give. When you are touched by the heart of the Father, you become a giver yourself.

In adulthood, my primary identity became that of a pastor rather than Father God's child. If my primary needs of belonging, provision, protection, or significance weren't met, insecurity and anxiety flared up. If someone didn't give me an exuberant compliment when I finished preaching, I was devastated. If the church board decided not to increase my annual salary, I was offended. Only when I finally understood my foundational identity as God's child did I find immovable, unshakable security.

What are the consequences when we cultivate our primary identity in anything other than Father? I've met wealthy Christian CEO's who cower in insecurity in the boardroom because they aren't drawing from their primary identity as God's child. In contrast, I've known a faithful Christian stay-at-home wife with four children and an alcoholic, adulterous, unemployed husband who walks in beautiful confidence in God's provision because her identity is centered around her Father.

This reminds me of a conversation Jesus once had with a rich young ruler (Matthew 19:16-24). The young man asked Jesus what good thing he could do to enter God's Kingdom. To his knowledge, he'd obeyed all of God's commandments and done all the right spiritual things. But like the popular U2 song, he "still had not found what he was looking for."

Seeing the young man's heart and sincerity, Jesus felt compassion for him. He went on to advise the rich young ruler to sell all he had and follow Jesus. Why sell his possessions? Like a child, the rich young ruler needed to pursue a living reliance on his heavenly Father for his core provision needs rather than counting on his own wealth. Sadly, the young man couldn't break away from an orphan Hoarder mindset enough to surrender his possessions and ended up walking away with his great wealth intact but never knowing the relationship of a beloved, cared-for son with a loving Father-Provider.

FROM HOARDER TO GIVER

If you've struggled with hoarding socially, financially, or physically in your life, you know how difficult these habits, thoughts, and actions are to break. In my own experience, the shift grew as my relationship with God as my Father-Provider began healing my heart insecurities. His goal? To be the sole source of provision for my every need so I would learn how to steward his blessings for the impoverished world around me. As I began walking with my Father, amazing peace about my financial needs rose up inside me. I had never experienced so much rest about finances before.

The shift started almost immediately after my life-transforming Father encounter in 2011. Over the following months after my two counselling sessions, I had some unusual dreams regarding Father God's bountiful provision. In one dream, I was whipping up scrambled eggs when I suddenly dropped a carton of eggs on the floor, leaving a mess of raw egg and fragmented shells. I anxiously scurried about trying to scoop the broken eggs off the floor, attempting to invoke the "five-second rule" so as not to waste food.

But the harder I tried, the worse the mess became and the more anxious I grew. At that moment, I discovered my wonderful Father God leaning down over me. Cheerfully, he told me, "David, don't bother with that. Just get some fresh eggs!"

Leading me to the pantry, he opened the door. Inside, I saw a walkway lined with shelving that was filled with countless thousands of eggs of all colors and sizes stretching as far as the eye could see. I turned to meet Father God's playful gaze. He nodded. "Of course, David, take as many as you want!"

There is something about having a relational exchange that rote memorization of scripture or doctrine cannot replace. I awoke from that dream with a deep-felt happiness, freedom, and security. This was the beginning of learning to lean into my heavenly Dad for provision unlike any way I had done in the past.

My prayers also changed. Instead of asking for specific financial needs, I began asking Father God what his provision story was for my life so I could come into agreement with it. In consequence, I began worrying less about financial or provision questions. As security grew in me that all my needs were already taken care of by my Father, it became more natural to ask God how should I invest my time and money.

A specific example of how Father God lovingly confronted my heart in this area arose in 2011. The context was how I'd handled a business friendship back in 2008 while I was still a full-time pastor. A college friend had invited me to conduct conflict management training for his company. My church board had allowed me to do this work alongside my pastoring responsibilities. Seeing my college friend develop a highly successful business encouraged me to start my own training company a few years later.

> There is something about having a relational exchange that rote memorization of scripture or doctrine cannot replace.

The Bible indicates wealth-building gifts come from God (Deuteronomy 8:18), so what could be wrong with this aspiration? The problem was that my approach was tainted by a Hoarder mindset. My motivations weren't focused on how I could bless others by acquiring wealth but with how much money I could accumulate for myself. Though I prayed to God for blessing, I can honestly admit I didn't involve him in the nuts and bolts of how I could build wealth in a godly fashion. In typical orphan Hoarder fashion, my goal was to become a "self-made man."

Then in 2011 as I was launching my own training company, I had a disturbing dream. In the dream, I was holding a secret meeting with one of my college friend's employees to try to acquire and copy his business model. When I woke up, I recognized immediately that, like Jacob, something was crooked in my motives. I wasn't trusting Father God to be my source of provision. Instead, I'd fixated on my friend's success, coveting it for myself.

Ignoring Father God's gentle warning, I launched my training business anyway, wrapped up in my own vision of financial breakthrough. I quickly lost thousands of dollars. Four months later, staring at an empty bank account, I felt bewildered and lost. Clouded by irritation and frustration, I wondered where Father God had been when I needed him. Why hadn't Father God stopped me? Or at least warned me I would lose my shirt?

After a month, I took an afternoon to myself. Alone with Father God, I spent time pouring out my simple questions. My heart melted as my Dad reminded me of the dream he'd sent me. Conviction set in as I realized that my default mindset was trying to meet my own core provision needs on my own. Recognizing my Hoarder propensity, I repented and stepped back from this business venture. The entire situation taught me that my greatest protection, financially and in every other area, was inviting my heavenly Father to meet my core needs before I made decisions.

A few months after my humbling business failure, I had a dream of myself on a roof with many other roofs in front of me. Behind me, Father God's voice rang out. "Run, David, and don't stop moving!"

I took off running and jumping from roof to roof. The only challenge was keeping my momentum and speed to make each jump to the next roof. When I woke up, I shared the dream with my wife. After praying together, we began to discern that God might be calling us to jump off the roof of our traditional church pastoral salary. In 2013, I prayerfully made the decision to remain in pastoral ministry but relinquish my salary.

Leaving a secure annual salary turned out to be the easiest thing I've ever done. Svea and I now required a creative source of income to provide for our household needs while leaving available time to minister in our church community. As a forty-year-old pastor with four children, a wife, and no income, I should have been anxious. But Father God continued to fill me with security. He also began opening doors I could never have opened by my own efforts.

Within a month, I started to see opportunities drawing on my educational background to consult for organizations like government, healthcare, and banking. Amazingly, I was invited to share with boards, managers, and CEOs on how to lead people with honor. Through training, coaching, and prayer, I witnessed Father God's presence spreading like an umbrella over my client organizations.

By 2015, Svea and I had stepped away from formal pastoral leadership within our church. Our family moved into an exciting faith adventure speaking and teaching at Bible/mission schools, camps, and church retreats. I continued consulting for governmental, financial, and telecommunications organizations, which covered some of our living and ministry expenses.

Father God works so differently than us, and we've come to appreciate his provision through many diverse sources. We've received anonymous gifts from people who want to support and cheer our family on in our ministry adventures. We've found money left in our van at night. Friends and even total strangers have dropped off money and left groceries at our door as well as clothing for our daughters. In 2015 alone, our first year of living in this unconventional dependence on our Father, we received over a hundred unexpected gifts of provision for our family.

Trust me, this is an adventure worth living! But it is only possible to enjoy when our security comes from our heavenly Dad. A few years ago, Svea and I were celebrating our anniversary on a weekend getaway to a hotel in Winnipeg. We were also seeking God for direction involving our financial situation. Little did we know Father God had a provision surprise to reassure us of his generous care.

Over the eighteen-hour period we were in Winnipeg, three individuals we'd never met before lavished us with treats. First, our table server unexpectedly paid for our $120 anniversary dinner at Cibo's, a high-end restaurant. Later that evening, the barista at a coffee shop insisted on presenting us with a free $25 dessert. The next morning, our server at International House of Pancakes insisted on paying for our $30 brunch. By the end of our weekend, Svea and I were both in tears as we felt the lavish love of our Father's care resolving the nagging money questions and future uncertainties.

Do you know what your heavenly Dad's provision story is for you? Do you struggle with scarcity thinking? Do you strive, get anxious, or even manipulate situations to obtain material possession or friends? Or are you happy when your friends prosper even more than you do?

Your Dad's love and affection will bring you more rest than a billion dollars. So go ahead and say to him now, "Dad, I need to know what your provision story is for me. I'm tired of trying to meet my own needs. Please show me how to rest in your provision. Help me, Dad!"

REFLECTIONS

- The Giver Impact Driver looks for opportunities to resource and give because of the overflow of content received in their life with Father God.

- Living day-to-day secure in a relationship with God as our Father shifts our view in any situation from that of lack or stagnation to that of possibility and hope.

- A whole new world of possibility opens up when we live life as we are—Father God's little child.

QUESTIONS TO CONSIDER

- Which Giver characteristic have you seen most often in your life?

- What crisis, challenge, or problems around you would benefit from your Father's giving drive operating in and through you?

- Which primal needs does your Father need to touch to give you more freedom to dream?

CONNECTING WITH MY FATHER

May I invite you to join me in praying the following prayer.

"Father God, I worship you as the ultimate Giver. Thank you for giving Jesus. Everything I have is a gift from you. Please teach me the care-free ways of being your little boy/girl. I want to grow into who I am in Jesus. I surrender to the exciting adventures of walking into any type of lack with you, my little hand in your big hand. I trust you. In Jesus's name, amen!"

CHAPTER SEVENTEEN

Your Adoption Support

*I*f you've made it this far in the book, some of you may be overwhelmed by a sense of where to start. Other readers may feel that this is all good but not hitting home in any powerful way. Some may have come from abusive homes, been abandoned by parents, or neglected by caregivers. Others may feel, "Hey, I've already got this. I learned about God as my Father years ago."

Wherever your journey originates, I pray that the following chapters will help move you into an upgrade in your Father-son or Father-daughter relationship. If you find yourself slipping into spiritual orphan mindsets or feelings of disconnect with God as your Daddy, there is an answer. In truth, we often accept unquestioningly God's amazing handiwork of transporting us from death to life. Yet we find it difficult to believe, encounter, and live intimately dependent on God as our very own Dad. God knew this would require his help. Jesus sacrificed himself to introduce us to his Father and ours, not just so we may enjoy eternal life but also so that our insecurities, anxieties, striving, and emptiness could be eradicated, enabling us to thrive in the here and now as sons and daughters of God.

As I've grown in learning to be a son of God, I've recognized how many lies about God, the church, and myself are rooted in not knowing my new place in God's family. As a pastor, I struggled with trying to build unity among believers and churches. I found myself rolling my eyes in frustration at the thousands of denominations, church splits, and schisms among the very people claiming to have God's love for the world. Perhaps you've felt the same.

> I've recognized how many lies about God, the church, and myself are rooted in not knowing my new place in God's family.

But once I encountered our Father, I experienced a wellspring of hope surging inside of me as I came to know the reality of my Dad's heart for his family. His love is greater than our biggest weaknesses. It will conquer every fear, bitterness, and broken situation. When Jesus preached that the kingdom of God had arrived on earth (Matthew 3:2; 4:17; 10:7; Mark 1:15; Luke 10:9; 17:21), he wasn't describing a bureaucratic operation but a family business (Luke 12:32). If you or I feel disjointed, disconnected, or disillusioned with Christianity or God's Kingdom, maybe we just aren't seeing God's family from our Father's reality.

So exactly what is my new place in God's family. It is that of adoption. In human terms, we might say that Jesus is the biological offspring while we have been adopted in and given the position as sons, daughters, brothers, sisters to our adoptive Father and Brother. And like a child adopted into a human family, this makes us co-heirs and gives us equal inheritance with our adoptive Brother, Jesus

Christ. Doesn't that just blow your mind? It certainly does mine!

> God sent him [Jesus] to buy freedom for us who were slaves to the law, so that he could **adopt us as his very own children**. And because we are his children, God has sent the Spirit of his Son into our hearts, prompting us to call out, "Abba, Father." Now you are no longer a slave but God's own child. And since you are his child, **God has made you his heir**. (Galatians 4:5-7)

> So you have not received a spirit that makes you fearful slaves. Instead, you received God's Spirit when he **adopted you as his own children**. Now we call him, "Abba, Father." For his Spirit joins with our spirit to affirm that we are God's children. (Romans 8:15-16; see also 8:23; 9:4)

> God decided in advance to **adopt us into his own family** by bringing us to himself through Jesus Christ . . . furthermore, because we are united with Christ, **we have received an inheritance from God**, for he chose us in advance, and he makes everything work out according to his plan. (Ephesians 1:5, 11).

A key to truly knowing God's family reality is understanding what adoption means to God through his Word. And since these biblical passages were originally written by the apostle Paul almost two thousand years ago in the context of the Roman empire, let's consider what adoption meant to the first century Christians who first heard this amazing truth. Broadly speaking, in Roman times adoption was a sober, costly, and lengthy process whereby a child became a legal heir recognized as son or daughter of the adopting father. The realities of Roman adoption have mind-blowing implications, so get ready to smile!

ADOPTION REALITY #1

Roman Law: When a child was adopted into a Roman family, they automatically had their entire past debts forgiven. Regardless of ethnicity, types of debts, or size of debts, all debt was completely wiped out. This might seem trivial in our day, as what kind of debt could a child have? But in Roman times, children were often sold as slaves to cover their parents' debts and were held responsible for parental debt.

Nor were adoptive sons and daughters necessarily young children, since a main purpose for adoption was to provide an heir. Caesar Augustus, the Roman emperor when Jesus was born (Luke 2:1) was eighteen when he was adopted by Julius Caesar to place him in the line of succession as heir to the throne. Whatever the age, any debts accredited to an adoptive child by law could not be carried into the adoptive family situation.

Our Life: If we are believers, one hundred percent of our sins and debts were paid for by Jesus. The very last words Jesus spoke on the cross were, "It is finished" (John 19:30). The literal Hebrew phrase, *tetelestai*, was the same stamped on a receipt when a debt was paid, meaning "paid in full." Our Saviour's blood-soaked signature ratifies our freedom from sin's debt—past, present, and future. In consequence, we can't bring our debts into our new family reality. As God's child, we live in a debt-free reality. No more shame, obligation, or condemnation.

ADOPTION REALITY #2

Roman Law: When a child was adopted into a Roman family, they automatically inherited the family name. In this context, the bequeathing of a name was considered a great honor. The new family member now represented their family's name, which in turn was key to the adopted child accessing whatever influence, resources, and authority the adoptive family possessed. For this reason alone, considering adoption was a serious matter for a Roman household.

Our Life: The name of Jesus is the most powerful name in the universe (Philippians 2:9-10). Jesus has promised that whatever his followers ask the Father in his name, he will do it (John 14:14; 16:23). Jesus commissioned us to bring new family members into his family through the name of the Father, Son, and Holy Spirit (Matthew 28:19). God's adopted children are reminded that whatever we do or say should be done in Father God's family name (Colossians 3:17).

ADOPTION REALITY #3

Roman Law: A newly-adopted child with Roman citizenship completely took on the identity of their new family. The adoptee was honored with inclusion in the lineage, history, and traditions of their adopted family. After completion of the public adoption ceremony, the adopted child was viewed and treated differently by everyone. In other words, they were now seen through the lens of their new family identity.

Our Life: As God's children, we are citizens of heaven (Philippians 3:20). God declares us to be new beings in Christ, our past completely gone and no longer able to define our future (2 Corinthians 5:17). Past broken beliefs and traditions have no place in our lives because they do not reflect who we really are. In short, Satan shudders to know who you really are (Revelation 12:10). Creation waits for you to know who you are (Romans 8:19). God knows who you are (Romans 8:16). The question is, do *you* know who you are?

ADOPTION REALITY #4

Roman Law: Adoption was a final, binding procedure. In Roman times, infanticide was not uncommon. If an infant was born of the wrong sex, had a birth defect, or was simply an unwanted extra mouth to feed, it was acceptable to discard the infant in a river or expose them to the elements to die. Unlike natural birth, adoption allowed adopting parents to know what they were getting. It was assumed that parents would thoroughly investigate and consider a potential adoptee before making any decisions. Once completed, parents were held responsible for their decision, making adoption unchangeable and final.

Our Life: Father God has investigated adoption options since the beginning of time (Ephesians 1:4). He knew us before we were born (Jeremiah 1:5). He promised he would never leave us nor abandon us, no matter how much we may fall, fail, or flounder (Hebrews 13:5). Our Dad's love for us is eternal, meaning it never dies, never gives up, and never fails (Jeremiah 31:3). It is forever.

ADOPTION REALITY #5

Roman Law: By Roman law, an adoptee was as much an heir to the estate as a biological son or daughter. Furthermore, birth of the child, not death of the parent, constituted estate inheritance. So the heir(s) had joint responsibility of their inheritance with their father while the father was still alive. Of course the father had absolute authority over everything in Roman culture. But unlike Jewish law, inheritance could be passed on even during the father's lifetime depending on how well the child was trained to take responsibility of estate responsibilities.

Our Life: Considering that Jesus is the biological son of our Father, it is amazing that we are joint heirs with him of earth, heaven, and the cosmos (Romans 8:17). And since we are heavenly heirs and have access to our inheritance right now, imagine what awesome opportunities we are being given. No wonder Jesus taught his disciples to pray, "Our Father who is in heaven . . . your kingdom come, your will be done on earth as it is in heaven" (Matthew 6:10).

This means that regardless how long we've been in God's family, whether a few hours, days, months, or years, we are now invited to walk with our Father, who wants to give us heavenly responsibilities and resources to transform our universe. God is not using this adoption metaphor conveniently or selectively. It is an actual reality paid for by our older Brother Jesus. Right now, you and I have access to heaven's resources because we are God's children. No wonder Scripture marvels:

> Look with wonder at the depth of the Father's marvelous love that he has lavished on us! He has called us and made us his very own beloved children. (1 John 3:1 TPT)

These facts alone should make Christians the most happy, optimistic, loving people on earth. As I grew into walking with my Dad, I found myself satisfied enough to be jovial, secure enough to dream again, and safe enough to love others unconditionally. Nothing in my circumstances had changed. Yet deep inside me, a swelling of supernatural security was overtaking every other reality in my life. I also found myself yearning for the Father's training, discipline, and mentoring so I could learn how to live with greater heavenly responsibilities, applying supernatural resources to every earthly situation.

A GOOGLE SCALE OF CHANGE

Almost everyone has heard of the internet search engine called Google. The word itself is derived from a number spelled *googol*. Coined by a nine-year-old back in the 1930s, the term googol represents the number one followed by a hundred zeros. That is a huge number! How huge? Mathematicians believe a googol is bigger than all the atomic particles in our universe combined. While such a number may be mind-boggling, I don't think it compares to the scale of change we go through when receiving God's gift of adoption into his family. To put it bluntly, the scale of change is astronomical!

Just think about it. It means moving from being dead in sin, without identity, and without hope to instantaneously being raised from the dead, adopted as a son or daughter into the Creator of the universe's family, and having the God of all as our loving, ever-present, personal Dad (Romans 6:1-11; Ephesians 2:1-10; Colossian 2:13-15). This type of change is so huge that it takes supernatural help to grasp and experience. I am continually amazed and giddy at how much I am constantly learning about my Dad and how to walk with him here on earth.

One inadequate example is a news story I remember reading years ago. In 2009, two orphan brothers were found living in a cave on the outskirts of Budapest, Hungary. Destitute with no friends or foreseeable future, the brothers survived by scavenging junk to sell for food. Then one day, lawyers from Germany showed up at their rocky haven to inform the brothers that they'd just inherited an estate worth more than six billion dollars. Their mother had cut off all relationship with her wealthy family, so when she died, the brothers had no idea they were in line to inherit a fortune. But under German law, direct descendants were automatically entitled to inherit the estate.

Imagine one day you're struggling to find a few dollars to buy food and the next day you find yourself presiding over a multi-billion-dollar estate. Sounds exciting, right? But though a huge blessing, these brothers would have required training and support to learn how to manage such a massive change. Not only is there an enormous learning curve for understanding the logistics, laws, planning, and consequences involving in managing billions of dollars, but there is also the internal grounding, impulse control, and values necessary to bear such a large responsibility without destroying your personal world. After all, statistics indicate that up to seventy percent of lottery winners eventually declare bankruptcy after winning that big pot of gold.

I love all of my daughters, enough to give my life to save any one of them. But imagine if for their fifth birthday, I handed one of these sweethearts the keys to my van with the suggestion, "Happy birthday, sweetie! Why don't you take the van for a spin? See if you can get it up to ninety miles an hour. Pick up some friends, and go celebrate your birthday!"

That type of permissive behavior is not true parental love. I am so grateful our Father is not that kind of dad. On the contrary, he loves us so much that he disciplines and trains us so the amazing blessings coming our way don't destroy us, as the author of the New Testament epistle to the Hebrews reminds:

> Let God train you, for he is doing what any loving
> father does for his children. Whoever heard of a son
> who was never corrected? (Hebrews 12:7, TLB)

You may not be consciously aware of it, but if you are a believer, you are living twenty-four/seven with a heavenly family. Your Brother Jesus, your heavenly Dad, and his Holy Spirit presence are with you wherever you go. Along with forgiveness of sin and redemption from death, you are inheriting something beyond comprehension, the privilege of reigning as co-heirs with Christ over the cosmos right now (Romans 5:17, 21; 2 Timothy 2:12; Revelation 22:5). That is a huge amount of authority and responsibility. Trust me, you will require some supernatural help to believe, receive, and walk as an adopted son or daughter of the King of kings!

REFLECTIONS

- Our unconditional adoption in God's family frees us from the debt of sin, giving us a new name, identity, inheritance, and an everlasting companionship with our God who is the Father, the Son Jesus, and the Holy Spirit.

- As God's children, we have such a huge inheritance that we require supernatural training and support to be able to live with and enjoy it.

QUESTIONS TO CONSIDER

- Which of the five adoption realities listed in this chapter have you least understood?

- How has this affected you?

CONNECTING WITH MY FATHER

May I invite you to join me in praying the following prayer.

"Father God, thank you for adopting me to be your son/ daughter. I humbly accept; that means I'm completely forgiven of all sin. I also accept that I have a new life and new identity and that I now carry the family name, Jesus, as my own. Thank you for making me your heir. The inheritance I have access to is beyond my comprehension. Therefore, please help me to learn and grow in this amazing gift. I trust you to mentor me in how to live on this earth. In Jesus's name, amen!"

CHAPTER EIGHTEEN

A Whole Family Affair

*I*n the months following my incredible encounter with Father God, I came to understand how each member of the Trinity works together to restore, train, and sustain us in learning how to walk as God's kids. During one late-night communication of joy and wonder with my heavenly Dad, I asked, "Father God, how does the Trinity help me here on earth?"

Father God showed me that my adoption required learning a new identity, a new way of seeing myself. He also showed me that since Adam and Eve first sinned, God's commitment to rescue humanity and restore us to our intended position as his sons and daughters has always been a heavenly family effort. I am so grateful for the joint support of Jesus, the Holy Spirit, and Father God in this transformation process.

How do we see the Trinity at work in our lives? First, Jesus dealt with the sin issue on the cross, restoring our **position** as God's children and giving us a new identity. The Holy Spirit supports our God-given **mission** on earth by empowering us, teaching us, and helping us. But it is our heavenly Dad who speaks so gently to the **conditions** of our hearts as his children. Regularly connecting with him fills our emotions and mind with security that only a Father can give, protecting us from accepting false identities for ourselves.

Maybe you are like me, priding ourselves on flying by the seat of our pants. But in truth, most tasks require a plan if they are to be accomplished successfully. The larger the goal, the larger the plan. The more that is at stake, the more thought and detailed planning is usually required.

I am so glad our Father God is the Master Planner of the universe. From the moment Adam and Eve sinned, God began outlining his plan for redemption through Christ (Genesis 3:15). Thousands of years later after hundreds of detailed prophecies laid out in God's Word, God's Son Jesus showed up at the perfect time in history, fulfilling a plan millennia in the making. But Father God's planning isn't just for the universe in general. He has a specific, individualized, perfect plan for each of our lives. An inheritance, purpose, and destiny he laid out for each of his sons and daughters before we were even born, as the apostle Paul reminded the Ephesian church.

> For we are His workmanship [His own master work, a work of art], created in Christ Jesus [reborn from above—spiritually transformed, renewed, ready to be used] for good works, which God prepared [for us] beforehand [taking paths which He set], so that

we would walk in them [living the good life which He prearranged and made ready for us]. (Ephesians 2:10, AMP)

When we don't have a close, conscious personal relationship with our Father God, we are also blind to Father God's thoughts, feelings, and plans for us. The apostle Paul understood the urgency of truly knowing our heavenly Dad. This is why his prayer for believers in his epistle to the Ephesian church (Ephesians 1:17-22) asks the Father to impart the wisdom and revelation of his Holy Spirit to help us know Father God more intimately and deeply.

I keep asking that the God of our Lord Jesus Christ, the glorious Father, may give you the Spirit of wisdom and revelation, so that you may know him better. (Ephesians 1:17, NIV)

Why does Paul pray this? Because he knows that even believers who seem to be doing well spiritually absolutely need the Holy Spirit's help to know their Father intimately. God's plan for you is an adventure! I can tell you that from my own experience. Why? Because you are important to him. You matter to Father God's heart.

And experiencing your Father's delight in you will affect everything else in your life. Meaningful connection with your Dad is the foundational key to unlocking God's eternal, personal, progressive plan and inheritance for you. Notice that Paul goes on to pray that our hearts will be illuminated, not just so we can know our Father more intimately, but so we can know the "glorious inheritances" he has given us.

I pray that the eyes of your heart may be enlightened in order that you may know the hope to which he has called you, the riches of his glorious inheritance in his holy people, (Ephesians 1:17-18, NIV).

...you have received a spiritually alive inheritance of glorious proportions from your Father, who is the Creator of the entire universe.

We've already discussed in brief the inheritance God's children share as co-heirs with Jesus. But what exactly is an inheritance? We tend to think of it in terms of transmitting possessions and property from parent to child, whether at a parent's death or while the parent is still living. But inheritance also involves transmitting DNA and personal traits to one's offspring. In his prayer, Paul highlights one of those personal traits in particular.

I also pray that you will understand the incredible greatness of God's power for us who believe him. This is the same mighty power that raised Christ from the dead and seated him in the place of honor at God's right hand in the heavenly realms. (Ephesians 1:17-20)

As God's child and heir, you have received a spiritually alive inheritance of glorious proportions from your Father who is the Creator of the entire universe. Just consider the scale of your inheritance. Our planet is almost eight thousand miles in diameter with a circumference of almost twenty-five thousand miles. That's huge! But you could fit a million Earth-sized planets into our sun. And you can fit a billion suns the size of ours into the largest known star of our universe.

This might explain why the apostle Paul prays so passionately for God's immeasurable, immense, and mighty power to be transmitted into our lives. Our inheritance in Christ is so enormous that it will take this kind of power to help mature, develop, and prepare us. Thankfully, it just so happens that our Father has more than enough power to carry and transform our weakness, brokenness, and frailty, and he loves doing this for his children.

SPIRIT OF ADOPTION

So if a deep, intimate relational connection with Father God is key to our inheritance, what do we do if we feel locked up, distant, or unable to relate to our Dad? Allow me to introduce you to the Helper, God's Spirit of adoption in you.

At the Last Supper, having told his disciples plainly that he would be leaving them and returning to heaven, Jesus comforted his disciples with the assurance that he would not be leaving them alone and abandoned.

> And I will ask the Father, and He will give you another Helper (Comforter, Advocate, Intercessor—Counselor, Strengthener, Standby), to be with you forever—the Spirit of Truth, whom the world cannot receive [and take to its heart] because it does not see Him or know Him, *but* you know Him because He (the Holy Spirit) remains with you *continually* and will be in you. (John 14:16-17, AMP)

You may perhaps think of the Holy Spirit in terms of being your Helper, Comforter, Advocate, and/or Counselor as the above scripture describes. But did you know Father God also sent the Holy

Spirit to help us grow into our adoption? To show us what it means to be his child, a prince or princess of the King of the universe?

> So you have not received a spirit that makes you fearful slaves. Instead, you received God's Spirit when he adopted you as his own children. Now we call him, "Abba, Father." For his Spirit joins with our spirit to affirm that we are God's children. (Romans 8:15-16)

Did you get that? The Holy Spirit your Father sent to earth, his Presence, committed to helping teach us (John 14:26) and guide us (John 16:13), testifies to you that you are adopted as God's very own child. Do you ever feel inadequate in connecting with God as your Father? Stop trying. Jesus said that the Helper, the Spirit who lives in you, is present to help you. All you need to do is ask him.

I really began learning about the Holy Spirit as my ever-present Friend when I was twenty-one years old and working a summer job as a painter. As I spent time with the Holy Spirit, I was amazed to discover he wasn't just an innate cloud, mist, or wind that blew into a room, leaving people overcome by emotion. He was a Person with thoughts, feelings, and desires who wanted to walk with me, talk with me, and lead me into truth.

As I grew in relating to the Holy Spirit, I experienced a list of sensations manifesting in my body. My legs, arms, and sometimes my whole body would tingle. If I continued conversing with the Holy Spirit, the tingling would grow until my whole body was numb. Accompanying these physical symptoms was a deep peace in my mind and heart.

At the time, I'd just finished my first year of undergraduate study in psychology and conflict resolution. Having studied psychosomatic symptoms, I began questioning whether some of my "manifestations" might have been induced by the suggestions of my mind rather than a genuine experience of the Holy Spirit's presence. I will never forget one morning during my devotion time when the Holy Spirit nudged me to randomly flip the calendar forward and mark any day with an invitation to him.

I am not a calendar person, so it took me a few minutes to even find one. But I dug one up and marked a day several months in advance. I then promptly tossed the calendar aside and forgot all about it. Months passed. I was painting a third-story apartment one morning when I felt a slight tingle in my hands. As I painted, the Holy Spirit's presence surged within me until it filled my whole body. Tears filled my eyes as I felt his love.

This continued throughout the day. As I returned home, I asked God what this could mean. He gently reminded me of the invitation he'd prompted me to record. I searched through my room for the calendar, finally finding it in my junk drawer. Flipping to the present month, I stopped in amazement. There on the current date was the scribbled invitation to the Holy Spirit I'd written many weeks before. I was astonished. My experiences with the Holy Spirit had indeed been real! He had responded to my invite. I had forgotten, but he had not.

Over the following years, I relied on the Holy Spirit for many things—understanding truth from God's Word, boldness to be a witness, and so on. But little did I know the Holy Spirit was yearning to lead me into a deeper encounter with my heavenly Dad. Not long after the calendar experience, a guest speaker at our church called me forward to share a prophetic word he felt God wanted me to hear. This was the same time period when I was going through a major personal breakdown and discouraged by conflict in our church, so I was so excited to receive an encouragement from God.

I guess I was hoping for promises of breakthrough, redemption, and healing. To my dismay, the man's words were something like the following: "David I'm proud of you. I'm walking with you even through things you don't understand. As you learn to follow me, you will go to places you haven't chosen. But I will be with you always."

The speaker started walking away, then turned to add, "David, there is something about your relationship with your Father that he wants to work on."

That last phrase bothered me, and I immediately dismissed it. Since I'd never rebelled against my earthly parents and had a great relationship with them, I automatically assumed I was doing well with Father God. Jesus had dealt with my sin and given me a new identity. The Holy Spirit was helping me grow in my faith and calling. Getting to know God the Father more fully would come about once I died and moved to heaven.

Years passed, and I forgot all about the prophetic word I'd received that evening. Then in 2011 when I began my new journey of pursuing God as my Father, the Holy Spirit reminded me of that prophecy I had received back in my early twenties. I was filled with awe as I realized the Holy Spirit had been offering even all those years ago to help me in my relationship with God as my Father. How valuable I was to my Father that his Spirit had been pursuing me throughout my life, working to introduce me to the affection in his heart for me.

Over the years, there were other examples of God's Spirit pursuing my heart for a meaningful Father-son relationship. I've mentioned the pressure I was facing to replace my father as senior pastor of my home church. The stress was disrupting my ability to sleep and eat, and I struggled with feeling betrayed and misunderstood by church leaders I'd trusted all my life, but who now seemed unwilling to listen to my convictions or accept my decision.

Then in 2011 just three months prior to my Father encounter, I had another dream. In my dream, I was standing in the middle of a circle of our church elders, feeling confused and trapped. Then I heard a voice say, "David, why do you look to these men for what only I can give you?"

When I awoke, the dream made no sense to me. But after I met my heavenly Dad three months later, the Holy Spirit revealed that the voice in the dream was Father God speaking to me. While it was healthy to have godly mentors in my life, it wasn't healthy to elevate their opinions, acceptance, and approval for the direction of my life above my heavenly Father's. Once I realized how I'd misdirected these relationships, I began directing questions of identity to my Father God, something I will share about in the next chapter.

> I've found that when my relationship with God is in order, my earthly relationships also tend to move towards order.

I've found that when my relationship with God is in order, my earthly relationships also tend to move toward order. In this case, the awesome benefits of giving honor to my Father's opinions about me released me to better see and truly honor these wonderful, godly church leaders who'd stood with me and mentored me my entire life. Being able to give heartfelt honor comes through seeing people and experiences from our Father's perspective. But before we can see and honor others, we need to see ourselves as he sees us.

REFLECTIONS

- Each person of the Trinity—Father, Son, and Holy Spirit—work together in our lives to restore us to the living reality of our new heavenly family status.

- The Spirit of Adoption lives inside of us, seeking to teach and guide us so our relationship with our Father can grow strong.

- Healing for our broken relationships comes by seeing others through our Father's eyes.

QUESTIONS TO CONSIDER

- Have you ever specifically invited the Holy Spirit to lead you in how to relate to God as your Father?

- Which broken relationships in your life would benefit from receiving your Dad's perspective?

CONNECTING WITH MY FATHER

May I invite you to join me in praying the following prayer.

"Father God, thank you for adoring me throughout my entire life even in ways I have not known. Please teach me what it means to be a member of your family. Lord Jesus, I worship you as my Savior. Thank you for pursuing my freedom before I was even born. Thank you for being an amazing Brother to me. I put my trust in you. Holy Spirit, I need your help to know who I am truly am. I need your power to rest in the finished work of Jesus so I can shine with my Father's love. I welcome you to help me in discovering who my Father is. In Jesus's name, amen!"

CHAPTER NINETEEN

Made For More

So, what do you feed on? What satisfies and keeps you energized? What is the daily fix you need first thing in your day (besides coffee)? The answer to those questions is how you live. Learning to live like Jesus is about learning to live as the Father's child. That requires a complete identity shift in every area of your life. So how does that happen? As with everything God does—through real, ongoing relationship.

Unlike any other living creature on earth, we were made as identity-seeking beings. God created our brains to constantly inquire, listen, and update how we see ourselves. Everything and everyone in our lives is wrestling to define who we are. A traumatic childhood experience. A broken relationship. Surfing Facebook. A tense board meeting. Television commercials. Newspaper articles. A church service. The list goes on. All of these are constantly sending signals to our hearts as to how we should see and relate to ourselves, God, and others.

The reality is that nothing in this universe can perfectly anchor you, define you, and free you to be yourself outside of your perfect heavenly Dad. Why? Because you came from him. You are his little boy or little girl, designed to receive definition from him. And I've learned in hanging out with our Dad that the best way to grow as a child is to ask him identity questions.

As our heavenly Dad's image bearer, we were designed to live life from the inside out.

What are identity questions? All of us, consciously or unconsciously, have at the core of our being deep questions unique to our personhood based around the same four identity molders we've discussed over and over: provision, belonging, protection, and significance. These are questions only our heavenly Father can answer. If they are left unanswered, we will frantically and restlessly strive to accomplish, prove, and gather successes, friends, and belongings to calm anxieties left by these unresolved needs.

We often forget we are human beings, not human doings, created in God's image. God identified himself to Moses as "I am that I am" (Exodus 3:14), not "I do that I do." In contrast, we tend to identify ourselves based on what we do. A typical question we ask a new acquaintance is "What do you do?" Our requests to God are often just a list of "doing" requests. "Lord, what am I called to do? . . . God, please help me accomplish the mission . . . Jesus, please help me to do your will."

While there is nothing wrong with these prayers, we lose critical opportunities for our Dad to teach us how to live out of our core personhood. As our Dad's image bearer, we were designed to live life from the inside out. I would even say we jeopardize our ability to realize his pleasure for our lives when we don't invite him to define our internal world. As Bill Johnson, a well-known minister in Redding, California, notes: "I can't afford to have thoughts in my head about me that God doesn't have in his."

Answers from your perfect, loving Father to the following questions will be truly transformative to how you see yourself and by extension how you live. Father God's definition of your unique, powerful personhood will make you immune to all other labels posted about you on social media, carelessly thrown at you by friends, or thoughtlessly pinned on you by family members. As we invite our Dad's perspectives into every area of our personhood, orphan shadow mindsets will literally disappear without any effort on our part. So let's check them out.

PROTECTION QUESTIONS

Living with orphan shadows leaves us feeling exposed, anxious, and defensive. In this state of identity, our automatic reaction is to resort to defensive posturing, avoidance of people, micromanaging others, offense-taking, and the list goes on. Have you seen these behaviors in your life?

If you have, remember that Father God wants to be your protection, your shield, and your fortress (Psalms 18:2; 91:2; 119:114). God has called us to be transformed by the renewing of our mind (Romans 12:2). So when you feel uneasy or exposed in a situation, I would encourage you to meditate on these scriptures and ask the Holy Spirit for other scriptures that speak of God's protection.

That said, our mind is made up of thoughts and feelings. So a complete renewal of our mind requires the emotional as well as the thinking side of our mind to experience truth. Imagine if I'd just adopted an eight-year-old girl who has only heard of me through her case worker and has yet to meet me. My biological daughter, also eight years old, has regularly experienced me—laughing, talking, playing together, crying on my shoulder for comfort, hearing my words of encouragement and love every day since she was born.

Now imagine I'm leaving on a week-long business trip. I write a personal letter to both my biological and newly-adopted daughter, promising that on my return I'll take them on a surprise outing, including fun activities, special gifts, and an exclusive restaurant celebration. Which daughter will be most impacted by my promises, waiting, imagining, and planning for my return? My biological daughter, of course. Why? Because she has experienced my love. She knows my father's heart through years of having her needs met. My newly-adopted daughter knows only my words of intent.

So too, deeper transformation includes renewal of the emotional side of our minds, not just the thought side. This involves experiencing Father God in real time through asking intimate questions about who we are or who he is. Some identity questions relating to protection include:

- Father God, what do you want to show me about your heart in this situation?

- "Father, where were you when ____?

- Dad, where are you in this situation?

- Father, what do you want to be for me this in this situation?

When possible, I ask these questions in the morning with my cup of coffee. Finding a quiet place without distractions is ideal, but as my adventure has grown in inviting Dad into these types of identity questions, I now ask him anywhere, anytime, finding immediate enriching feedback. Doing this regularly floods your heart with a deep security and peace, quietly dissolving those orphan shadows you've wrestled with for years.

In my early twenties, I was on a missions trip to Mexico while my younger brother Andrae was on an outreach trip in Nepal with YWAM (Youth With A Mission). One night in a dream, I saw Andrae being struck by a green truck while ministering at a busy Nepalese street corner. In my dream, I was flown back to Canada, where I was escorted with other tear-stained family members into a room containing a black body bag stretched out on a stainless-steel table. An official unzipped the bag, revealing my brother's cold, dead features. Anger seized me. Walking up to the body, I grabbed it, calling Andrae to return in Jesus's name. After several calls, my brother revived, gasping and coughing for air.

I awoke in a cold sweat, convicted I needed to pray for Andrae immediately. After pacing in the washroom, praying for protection, I finally went to bed. When we were both back home, I shared my dream. To my amazement, I learned that Andrae had been nearly run over by a green truck during the exact time period I'd been awakened to pray.

That is your Dad! He wants to help. More than that, he wants us to live in the peace of knowing as his children that we are safe. As we grow in this assurance, we can expand our Father's protection to those around us.

BELONGING QUESTIONS

Lying in the snow, I clutched my knee, screaming in agony. At nine years of age, I prided myself on being a fast runner. But my speed had resulted in slipping on ice and splitting my knee open on a jagged rock. I groaned in pain as my brothers ran to fetch my dad. Seeing him emerging from our home brought a wave of relief. As he came closer, what do you think I needed from him as a son?

He could examine my bloody gash, stand up with folded arms, and inform me, "Okay son, looks like you've cut through two of the three layers of skin, the epidermis and dermis. There are four stages of healing—red blood cells forming clots, white blood cells defending against infection, fibroblast cells dropping collagen into the wound, then the dermis and epidermis closing the wound. Based on this, I believe you have about six weeks of healing before you can run again."

Or he could scoop me into his arms, carry me to his vehicle, and drive me to the hospital, all the while reassuring me everything would be okay, praying with confidence and warmth in his voice, and expressing pride for me as his son. The second option is, of course, what actually happened. Notice that my dad related to my emotional needs before speaking to my mind. If this is what an earthly father does, how much more will our perfect Father extend belonging and care to us in times of insecurity.

Orphan shadows often manifest in a sense of unworthiness, abandonment, isolation, victimization, and feeling misunderstood. In this state of identity, our automatic reaction is to resort to performing, manipulating, exaggerating, conforming to other people's expectations, or doing whatever we can to create belonging for ourselves. Which of these behaviours have you seen operating in your life?

If you've been caught in this way of living, Father God wants you to know how valuable you are to him. He has literally been thinking happy thoughts about you every second since before time began (Psalms 17:8; 139:17-18; Isaiah 43:1; John 10:28). Meditate on these scriptures when you struggle with questions of belonging.

I find it so refreshing to reflect on how much my Father loves and enjoys me as an individual. God doesn't just love us en masse but celebrates each of us according to our unique personality, talents, and character as we are reminded in the parable of the Good Shepherd celebrating the rescue of his one lost sheep even though he has ninety-nine others (Luke 15:3-7). Ask God belonging identity questions such as:

- Dad, how do you feel about me right now?

- Father God, where do I stand with you?

- Father, how do you see me?

- Dad, what characteristics do you love the most about me?

When I ask these questions, Father God's answers are the most fulfilling response in the world. I might be able to carry on for awhile missing devotional or worship times. But I can't go too long without feeling the affection and belonging in my Dad's feelings toward me. Experiencing Father God's deep love keeps me grounded in security and belonging, regardless of my own circumstances.

Some readers may wonder if Father God will truly share his emotions in a way they can comprehend. Let me share the following true story as an example of how faithful our Dad is to share his heart with us. A girl named Tamara who attended our church youth group during my teens lived on a wheat farm outside our small community. For weeks she'd been struggling with depression, doubting if God really cared about her.

One crisp, cold autumn night shortly after harvest, Tamara walked out into her father's freshly-cut wheat fields. Stubble stabbed at her feet as she wandered across the fields. Stopping finally to look up at the bright stars amidst the black night sky, she cried out silently, "God, do you really care about me?"

She heard no response except the rustle of the cold breeze through the stubble and crickets chirping. But in that moment, she felt an internal nudge to look down. Something white was fluttering between her feet, caught under a clod of dirt. Bending down, she picked it up. It was a folded piece of paper. Heart racing, she unfolded the paper and read the words written across it: "I love you." Talk about a billion to one improbability! When Tamara shared her experience with the rest of us, she no longer doubted her heavenly Father cared about her!

Your heavenly Dad loves you, and he wants to answer the unconscious question every child carries: do I belong? He is actively pursuing your heart because he wants you to enter his rest (Hebrews 4:1). When I began letting Father God meet my needs for belonging, my level of rest skyrocketed. When I tapped into his heart for me, confusion became a distant memory. An anchor of peace beyond understanding flooded me. It doesn't matter how good or spiritual you are or what you accomplish. Those will never replace God's loving answer to your heart that you are his child and that you belong.

PROVISION QUESTIONS

While I love tossing a football ball around, I'll admit I'm also a bit of a romantic. As a teenager, I dreamed of what it would be like to marry a young woman who would also be my best friend. I imagined elaborate scenarios of surprising my future sweetheart with balloons containing amorous messages, trails of roses, eloquent poetry.

How many of us have unfulfilled dreams—an ideal job, owning a business, getting married, the perfect luxury home or car. While my own romantic dream of marrying a special friend was a deep-seated desire, I didn't know how to invite my Father into this part of my being. The result was years of needless insecurity and turmoil. No matter how hard I tried, I couldn't find a relationship that would catch momentum. Even worse, every relationship which went nowhere increased my self-hatred, frustration, and despair. I wish I'd known then that I could invite my heavenly Dad's perspective into the unconscious anxiety I carried about provision.

Eventually, I let go of my self-made mirage of marital bliss, trusting Father God to provide. I guess you could say I came to myself, realizing I was in the pigpen and needed to return home to my Father. Within months of this surrender, I laid eyes on my future beautiful, blond bride Svea dressed in black leather boots and a red dress speckled with white flowers. The memory still makes me smile.

I was twenty-seven years old, co-leading a YWAM missions leadership school in Colorado. Originally from California, Svea had grown up in a Christian home. After high school, she'd attended a YWAM discipleship training school (DTS), then finished her college education before returning to YWAM on staff. When I met her, she'd already spent several years leading DTS programs around the world and was currently on a year-long sabbatical. She lived a half-hour drive from the YWAM base but occasionally joined us for worship services. Listening to her pray filled me with respect for her, as I could see how much she loved God. Every time she entered a room, I was aware of her presence.

While I really wanted to initiate a date with Svea, I had no extra income or vehicle. So I began praying. Within days, someone who didn't even know about my growing interest in Svea offered me a vehicle to use. A day later, I received some funds that allowed me to invite Svea out on a date. We discovered that we had a lot in common, including sharing the same birthday.

This led to building a strong friendship, which blossomed eventually into a serious romantic relationship. I finally got to do the wild romantic gestures I'd imagined years earlier—filling her bedroom with balloons, sending her flowers when she was visiting family, surprises in public places, and so on. The ultimate romantic expression was my proposal. But as a young missions leader living on donations, I had no money to buy an engagement ring. Svea laughed at my concerns, assuring me that she'd happily marry me with nothing more than a rubber band on her finger.

But Father God had this covered too. Around this time, a missions supporter gave me a one-time donation of two thousand dollars. I was exuberant, assuming this was God's provision for my engagement ring. That hope blew up a couple days later when I was asked to fly to Thailand to help mediate a conflict in our mission. Since I had a degree in conflict resolution, I was the logical person to send, but the one catch was that I had to pay my own way. So this was God's intent in sending me two thousand dollars. Ouch!

I knew God wanted me to go, so I bought my plane ticket. My last day in Thailand, I'd finished mediating the conflict in question. Walking back to my hotel, I stopped at an internet café to check my email (yes, this was before you could check email on your phone!). To my shock, a man I didn't even know had emailed me, asking if I was in a serious relationship. If so, he had an engagement ring worth about twenty-five hundred dollars he wanted to offer me for free.

Stunned is the only word to describe how I felt. Excitedly, I responded, explaining my situation and how his email was truly God's miraculous answer to my prayers. Now I could plan a real marriage proposal with a real ring! God provided more unexpected funds, which allowed me to create an all-day romantic scavenger hunt. Each stop came with a red rose and a poetic clue to various memorable places in our relationship—the location of our first date, the church we attended, going up Pike's Peak, and so on.

The day ended at an upscale restaurant overlooking the Colorado Springs skyline. After our meal, I took Svea by the hand to walk along the outdoor patio. It was a clear moonlit night, and a breeze was gently playing with her blond hair. Glancing at the people visible through the restaurant window, Svea said teasingly, "We should give them something to look at."

"I agree." With a wide grin, I knelt down. Just that week, I'd received in the mail the engagement ring my generous donor had offered. Thanks to some judicious investigating, I knew Svea's ring size and style preferences, so I'd had the gorgeous diamond from the donated ring reset in a white-gold band I knew she wanted. I held it up.

"Svea, you are the most amazing person I have ever met. You are so beautiful inside and out. I cherish these last few months together, and I would be honored if I could spend many more years together with you. Would you do me the honor marrying me?"

Svea's beautiful features were alight with joy. "Yes, yes, of course, yes!"

Just then Svea stopped to stare at the ring now on her finger with an expression of absolute wonder. This was certainly no rubber band! "Wait, where did this come from? How did you get this?"

I am still amazed at how detailed my Father's provision was to me in this area of my heart. God is into details because his impulse as a loving Dad is to provide for us. As Jesus once reminded:

So if you sinful people know how to give good gifts to your children, how much more will your heavenly Father give good gifts to those who ask him. (Matthew 7:11).

Notice Jesus doesn't say *if* but *how* to give gifts. A loving father gives gifts, period. Our Father God knows how to provide for every need we have—social, physical, or financial. But how he does it isn't always the way we expect or ask. Why? Because like those car keys I don't give my five-year-old, our Dad knows how to give us good gifts that won't destroy us but bless us and others fully.

Learning to be a receiver in our relationship with our Father means being free of orphan shadows such as anxiety, helplessness, emptiness, and suspicion. If our identity grows out of these feelings, we will resort to comparison, striving, avoiding risk, and hoarding. If any of these behaviors are your ways of working through life, Father God wants you to know he gets what you need and he is going to provide for you (Jeremiah 29:11; Matthew 6:8; 7:11; James 1:17). Meditate on these scriptures, allowing them to transform how you think about your Father's intentions toward you.

But don't stop there. Take time to sit on your Dad's lap, trusting him to share his prospective on provision. Ask Father God provisions questions such as:

- Father God, how have you blessed me in the past?

- Dad, how do you see me in this situation?

- What do you want to be for me in this _____?

- Dad, what's your view of this need?

Of the four core needs, provision carries some of the biggest footholds of deception in our identity because provision, unlike other needs, often involves tangible results we depend on. Growing into the full authority of adoption means allowing your Dad to re-define how you see yourself providing for your life.

"But, David, I'm not the spiritual type who hears things from God!" you might say.

Does the wind blow? Do babies cry? As God's child, it is in your nature to hear your Father. He didn't create any deaf, blind, or mute sons or daughters. The key is to believe what Jesus says about you:

> Whoever believes in me, as Scripture has said, rivers
> of living water will flow from within them. (John
> 7:38, NIV)

Other biblical passages describe God's voice as the sound of many waters (Revelation 1:15; 14:2). Water is refreshing, moving, and spontaneous. The image is of water thundering over a waterfall, rushing over boulders, crashing as surf on a beach, or trickling gently in a narrow stream. As you plug into your heavenly Dad's heart, don't try to predetermine what kind of sound you will receive. Clear away distractions like cell-phones and TV. Be patient as distracting thoughts may bombard you.

As you settle in, a general atmosphere or specific thoughts and feelings will spontaneously flicker in your mind and heart. If what you receive is loving, patient, and peaceful, that is your Dad talking to you. Stay in that place. If you receive comments or pictures you don't understand, ask Father God what they mean. He wants to discuss things with you, laugh, and enjoy you. Relax and know your Dad is thrilled with you regardless of what happens.

SIGNIFICANCE QUESTIONS

"Why am I here? What is my purpose?" are questions human beings have been asking since Adam and Eve. If we don't allow Father God to answer those questions, we slide into orphan shadows of insignificance, destitution, boredom, confusion, and meaninglessness. So why are we here? What is our purpose?

You and I are more valuable to our heavenly Dad than we can imagine. We are eternally alive, standing in the center of a great story written by our very own loving Father. We are invited to help write his story through living a grand adventure as his sons and daughters on this earth. If you've chosen to believe in Jesus as your Savior, you are apart of Father God's family mission to redeem the world. In Christ, you are predestined for good works of helping, reconciling, advocating, and giving to a broken and fragmented world (Ephesians 2:10).

Father God's thoughts will bring meaning, purpose, and significance to your life (Psalms 139:13-14; Isaiah 60:1; Jeremiah 29:11; John 3:16; Ephesians 2:10). Meditate on these scriptures as you seek to have your thoughts aligned with his thoughts. Ask our Dad significance questions like:

- Father God, why did you create me this way?

- Dad, what do you think about me?

- Heavenly Father, what am I becoming?

- Dad, what about me is valuable to you?

Father God wants to infuse us with a sense of destiny that matches the special way he made us. Only one version of us will ever show up on history's stage. There are no duplicates, revisions, or copies. Nothing we acquire, give, or accomplish will quell our quest for meaning in life. The only key to understanding our purpose and significance as sons and daughters of the King is opening our heart to our loving Father God.

REFLECTIONS

- We miss our Father God's pleasure for our lives when we do not invite him to define our internal world.

- To grow in deeper authority as God's kids, we require his personal thoughts and feelings about core issues of belonging, protection, provision, and significance in our lives. His answers remind us of who we really are in Jesus.

QUESTIONS TO CONSIDER

- How much of your prayers with God are requests about tasks versus invitations for Father God to share how he sees you?

- Which identity questions (belong, protection, provision, significance) do you feel least grounded in?

- When looking at your life so far, do you know your Dad's personal and customized view of who you are?

CONNECTING WITH MY FATHER

May I invite you to join me in praying the following prayer.

"Father God, I believe there is so much more yet to discover in my relationship with you. I am only starting to realize that I am your treasured one and that you proudly stand with me as my Dad. I am in relationship with you not because of any goodness or determination of my own. It is all because of you—your powerful mercy and grace revealed in Jesus. I want to know your thoughts and feelings about who I am. Because you are my Dad, I need to know how you see me. Thank you for being my Dad. As your little one, I hold up my weakness and vulnerability to you. I love you with all my heart. In Jesus's name, amen!"

EPILOGUE

Wonderment

So what types of social cannibalism have you struggled with? Do you see Dictator tendencies tempting you to micromanage, meddle, or interfere to see your plans realized? Perhaps you've preferred the Loner approach of sitting back and judging others while avoiding real vulnerability and connection with other's hearts. Are you seeing any Slave leanings that fixate on performance, striving for acceptance through your own efforts or blindly idolizing someone who appears more successful? Have you fallen into a Hoarder mentality of scheming, comparing, or striving to provide for your own needs?

Our world is being pulled apart at the seams. Divorce, racism, polarization, sexism, corruption, and all kinds of dark pressures have, are, and will press down on our very humanity. Social, financial, and emotional cannibalism is rampant everywhere we look. The world needs heavenly sons and daughters to save it from insecurities and default strategies that only disable, divide, and destroy. Humanity's global orphanage needs a family reflecting what our loving Father looks like.

And that is precisely what we can be. Thanks to Jesus's death, burial, and resurrection, we have been eternally adopted into God's family. As a son or daughter of Father God, we carry his nature. Every orphan behavior has been exchanged for the characteristics of our Father as a Helper, Reconciler, Giver, and Advocate. Our "impact driver" as God's child is now to help, advocate, reconcile, and give to others.

Instead of controlling, we now move to serving others. In place of withdrawing from relationships, we move to bring people together. The impulse of grabbing for ourselves is replaced with a desire to meet others' needs. Instead of living as unworthy minions, we are able to raise our voice and fight for the weak and helpless.

Sounds too good to be true? The wonder of who we really are in Christ can indeed seem like an unattainable fairy tale until we learn how to connect, enjoy, and be helplessly reliant on our heavenly Dad. When coming to the end of writing this book, I asked Father God what title I should give the epilogue. Wonderment was the word God laid on my heart. Wonderment means a state of awed admiration or respect. It's that moment in time when everything stands still. When you feel absolute joyous contentment mixed with a single focus on the object of your affection.

Wonderment is what I felt in my own first intimate encounter with my heavenly Dad in that vision by the waterfall at the top of the cliff. Hearing his heart for me and healing my past changed me on every level. But I haven't yet shared the final part of my Father encounter. I left you where I'd frozen in fear, refusing to get into the dinghy with my Father because the waters seemed just too rough. So let me share the rest of that encounter now.

Without any rebuke, Father God gently grasped my hand. "David, let me show you something."

Peaceful bubbles of joy welled up inside me as I followed my Dad down a trail through pine trees. We stopped in front of a large building. Intricately carved wooden double doors loomed over me at least two stories high. Father God's eyes danced as he opened the doors.

"Okay David, I've got a surprise for you. This is called the war room. In the days ahead, you will be fighting battles that threaten your rest and trust in me. But you will never be alone. I will always be with you."

As we stepped indoors, I saw shelves from floor to ceiling on both sides filled with every kind of weapon and armour imaginable—broadswords, ornately decorated daggers, spears, tall and short shields, combat boots. Father God smiled at me. "Go ahead and pick a weapon for yourself, David."

Moving along the shelves, I examined different weapons, trying to decide which would be best for me. But I felt too overwhelmed at the vast assortment to make a decision. Finally, my Dad moved up beside me and laid his hand on my shoulder. "David, let me help."

Reaching deep into the shelf beside us, he pulled out a small, sparkly object. "David, this is your greatest weapon."

I was amazed to recognize what he was holding out to me. It was a shining gold chain from which hung a gold six-pointed "Star of David." When I was thirteen years old, I'd received my first prophetic message of encouragement from a visiting speaker. He'd stated that I carried a David spirit, someone who yearned to know God's heart (1 Samuel 13:14; Acts 13:22). He went on to instruct me never to change my human name. What was remarkable about this prophetic word is that the speaker didn't know me or that my name actually was David.

This had a profound impact on me. Some weeks later, I bought a Star of David necklace to commemorate how I believed God saw me. I wore the necklace for years until the life disappointments I've mentioned left me disillusioned as to my identity as Father God's son. It had been almost twenty years since I'd discarded that necklace.

Clipping the necklace around my neck, Father God continued, "Your identity, the one I give you, is the most valuable thing you can carry with you. You are my beloved. You delight my heart, David. Don't let anyone or anything take that away from you."

Tears dripped down my checks as I felt a wave of acceptance wash over me, followed by a deep sense of confidence in my purpose and significance. A wondrous sense of destiny I'd forgotten existed flooded me. I felt like a kid again.

Leading me back through the trees, Father God once again stopped beside the waterfall and yellow dinghy I'd seen when I first met him. With a grin, he prodded, "Are you ready for an adventure yet, David? Will you come with me now?"

I could hear the thundering roar of the waterfall. The river was still turbulent and dotted with sharp rocks. Violent waves continued to toss the little yellow dinghy as they surged toward the cliff edge. But this time without hesitation, I burst out, "I'm with you, Dad. Let's go!"

We climbed into the dinghy. As we bounced toward the steep drop-off, Father God reminded me, "I'm with you all the way!"

Our boat slid over the edge. But instead of crashing into the torrent below, we floated gently toward the shore. Great swells of belly laughter shook both of us as we touched down.

You were created for adventure. You were created to be loved, cherished, provided for, and protected by your heavenly Dad. Whether you've heard him or not, he still waits and calls for his little boy or girl. Start today. If you aren't sure how to start, ask the Spirit of Adoption for help. Ask Father God the questions you didn't realize were burning inside you. Let him speak to your deep needs. Let him name you.

As you do so, you will find yourself passing into a state of wonderment similar to when you first received Jesus into your life (or maybe you're already there!). At times I pinch myself, just realizing how very real and present this new life is.

Do I still experience hardship and challenge? Absolutely. But they are like distant meteors streaking across the night sky, viewed from the warm comfort of my living room chair. Experiencing my Father's fondness for who I am calms every worry.

Do I still struggle with different orphan shadow behaviours? I do. But even these are fading as my life's story continues to add experience after experience where Father God meets all my needs, continuously reminding me I am no longer an orphan. I am safe and secure with my Dad.

Peace, rest, and authentic love are always the fruit of being with Father God. So today I am also experiencing so much more enjoyment in my Christian journey as new impulses to advocate, give, reconcile, and help others bubble up in my heart. It's like Ann Voskamp, Canadian blogger and author, writes in her book *One Thousand Gifts: A Dare to Live Fully Right Where You Are*:

> Sometimes you don't know when you're taking the
> first step through a door until you're already inside.

As you step through the door, grabbing your Father's big hand with your tiny hand, you'll find on the other side a world of adventure and wonder. You'll walk a new way as sons and daughters of your

Creator. And you'll find the security, belonging, and significance your soul has been craving since the day you were born.

RESOURCES

An Overview Of The Model

What you've read to this point may perhaps seem a new concept. But in truth, it is not complicated. In fact, keeping things simple and relational is what becoming like a child is all about. The following model is intended to provide you with a clear, concise roadmap to understanding yourself and how to grow in your connection with Father God. The model is called the Impact Styles Inventory (I.S.I.). It shows the Orphan Shadow mindsets we have discussed, matched against the true reality of our Father God's Impact Drivers. A few points to keep in mind as you go through the model.

- Who you are, your eternal identity, is sealed in the finished reality of Jesus's death, burial, and resurrection. Inviting your heavenly Father into any epiphanies you may have about your behaviours aligning with a particular orphan shadow, is an appropriate and recommended application step.

- This model acts as a compass pointing you where to specifically invite your Father.

- While there may be some overlap between the different shadows or different drivers, your primary tendency will be the one you see most often during stress or crisis.

- How you pursue meeting your primal needs (belonging, protection, provision, significance) determines what shadow or driver you express in areas of your life.

- Resist the temptation to apply or diagnose other people's orphan shadows.

LIVING OUT OF OUR ADOPTION REALITY

When we encounter the Father and live in our adoption reality, he takes what was broken in orphan state and rebirths into something powerful, able to change the world around us. Orphan shadows fade.

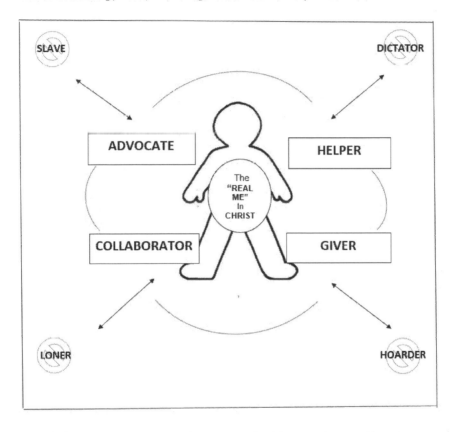

James 1:17 "Every good and perfect gift comes down from the Father of heavenly lights who does not change like turning or shifting shadows."

THE IMPACT STYLES OVERVIEW

DICTATOR Shadow	LONER Shadow	SLAVE Shadow	HOARDER Shadow
Controlling Judgmental Behavior	Isolation Vindictive Behavior	Performance Addiction Behaviors	Scheming Comparing Behaviors

HELPER Driver	RECONCILER Driver	ADVOCATER Driver	GIVER Driver
Serving Empowering Impulse	Forgiving Collaborating Impulse	Liberating Comforting Impulse	Supporting Sharing Impulse

INVITATION

Sharing my story has been invigorating, exhausting, and deeply fulfilling. If you were able to read your way to the end, I hope and pray there is a curiosity and maybe even wonder growing inside. Though I may not know you personally, if you are a follower of Jesus Christ, we are in the same family of God. You are my brother or sister in Christ. For that reason, it is my desire to serve and support any growing interest in the message of this book.

Over the years, I've been honored to meet multiple people impacted by the message of our heavenly Dad. God has been and is speaking through people around the world about the power of knowing our Father intimately. This is why Jesus came—to bring us back to our Dad. Now more than ever, a world raging with social cannibalism needs to know the security we can all experience in our Father and release into our world.

For this reason, I want to invite you to join other family members and together discover our Father God. We can reflect him by stepping out of our orphan shadows, learning to walk as his children, and being driven by his heart to impact others.

Go to areweallcannibals.com to access more resources. Any other online supports and additional resources will be shared there.

Thank you for partaking in my heart. I hope you will join us in this incredible adventure ahead.

See you soon,

David Braun

Made in the USA
Middletown, DE
06 June 2021